I'm Fine, Thanks

Chris Doveton

The Book Guild Ltd

First published in Great Britain in 2020 by
The Book Guild Ltd
9 Priory Business Park
Wistow Road, Kibworth
Leicestershire, LE8 0RX
Freephone: 0800 999 2982
www.bookguild.co.uk
Email: info@bookguild.co.uk
Twitter: @bookguild

Typeset in 11pt Minion Pro

Printed and bound in the UK by TJ International, Padstow, Cornwall

ISBN 978 1913208 851

British Library Cataloguing in Publication Data.
A catalogue record for this book is available from the British Library.

Contents

The Start

This is a love story. It is also a story of grief, destruction and redemption, of loss and ruin, also, of hope and faith. It is a story about how love in later life can save you.
Thank you, Pauline, for being that love.

My grateful thanks to Abby Aron and Hannah Droy for making this book possible

One

Prologue

MEN OF MY ERA ARE BORN WITH STIFF UPPER LIPS. WE
don't suffer depression, despair or grief. If we are knocked
sideways, or flattened on the ground, we shout 'jolly good'
and keep calm and carry on.

That was me. I used to inhabit an armour-plated world
where nothing could escape and no one could get in. But
one day, life threw me a curveball so all-encompassing
that it left me vulnerable, exposed and defenceless.
Survival depended on my owning up and admitting to the
world around me, that my stiff upper lip was, in fact, a
little droopy around the edges and that I needed all the
help I could get.

This is the story of how I tried, failed, tried, failed,
tried and eventually succeeded in detaching my heart
from its breastplate and shield and began wearing it on
my sleeve.

If I had not exposed the depths of my despair for all the world to see, I am certain that I would not be here to tell my story.

Two

Wedding Day

September 1965

We marry in autumn.

The bells of the Abbey chime.

Purcell's 'Trumpet Voluntary' bursts into life.

I wait nervously at the altar.

Murmurs signal Anne's arrival at the great West Door. I resist the urge to turn and watch as she sets forth down the aisle on the arm of her father, Vernon. I glance nervously at my brother, who offers, in return, an encouraging nod and reassuring wink.

His smile says it all. My bride is beautiful.

I close my eyes in anticipation as I wait for her. Standing there, under the magnificent vaulted ceiling of my beloved Bath Abbey, I get the sense, for the first time in my life, that everything is slotting into place. I am about to marry the love of my life.

It is time to put my past behind me and look forward to the future.

Anne laughs, giddy with champagne, as I carry her over the threshold, both of us heady with love.

Losing my balance, slightly, I almost drop her on the hallway floor. "Careful!" she says.

I pretend to drop her again.

She giggles and clasps me tightly.

"Chris! Stop!" she gasps.

I kiss her on the forehead and look deep into her eyes. I have found my kindred spirit. I feel so alive with optimism, with hope. I can't believe my luck. Together, we are about to embark on a journey through life, a life filled with shared love of foxtrots and cha-cha-chas, dogs, cats, and music.

I couldn't be happier.

"Welcome home, wife," I whisper.

Little can I imagine, as I lie her gently on the sofa, that this random act of innocent love will one day become an everyday part of life.

Three

Saint-Brieuc, Brittany

Summer 1987

ANNE STUMBLES AND LOSES HER FOOTING.

Louisa catches her arm.

"Whoops!" Louisa says, laughing lightly, helping her mother to steady herself. "Careful!"

Anne looks down at her sandals. She holds on to Louisa's hand for balance as she bends and tightens the Velcro strap across her instep.

I watch as they continue walking arm in arm towards the golden sandy beach ahead of me, chatting away as if nothing has happened.

The path is level and Anne is not a clumsy person. I had watched her put her sandals on that morning, smoothing the strap so the Velcro matched up perfectly. She had put on the sandal in the same graceful way she performed every task, with precision, care and attention. There is no reason for her stumble.

"Wait for me!" I call, running to catch up.

I put the small incident out of my mind – just an odd moment on an otherwise perfect day.

Four

Headache

1990

"Oh, Chris, please do stop making a fuss." Anne rubs her temples and closes her eyes.

"Maybe it's time *you* begin making a fuss!" I reply sternly, bending down to give her a kiss. "Is that another of your headaches starting? Let me get you a tablet."

I hand her a glass of water and a small bottle of paracetamol from her dressing table and notice it is half-empty. Already? I try to remember when I bought them. Last week?

I think back. It was when I went to the chemist, that sunny Saturday morning. Anne had been in such pain she had put her pillow over her eyes and asked me to close the curtains against the light. I hadn't bothered getting showered. I had thrown on my tracksuit and run down the hill to buy her some painkilling relief.

I look at the bottle again. That was a lot of paracetamol to take over five days.

I make no comment, close the door and go downstairs.

"I would like to make an appointment with Dr King, please," I say, quietly.

"The earliest slot will be next week Monday, will that do?" The receptionist sounds harried and busy.

"Yes, I suppose that will do, but if you have any emergency slots, we would like to take it. I am not sure my wife can wait for another week. She is in a lot of pain."

"Of course, Mr Harrison. I will call you if any free appointments come up."

The receptionist puts the phone down without waiting for my response.

"Are you free next Monday?" I ask, as I enter the dark bedroom with a cup of tea and a single triangle of toast laid out on a breakfast tray. I have learnt there is no point giving Anne a large breakfast when she has these bad head episodes.

"Why?" she enquires, wincing, as she hauls herself up in bed.

I place the tray on her knees. "I have made you an appointment with Dr King. We need to find out what is causing these headaches."

Anne sighs. "Chris, I told you not to fuss? Fussing includes making an appointment with Dr King. You do know the visit will be a total waste of time. He's completely hopeless. Anyone who prescribes lemon and honey for throat cancer deserves to be struck off. Poor Mary."

"That was just a one-off. Anyone can make a mistake. I haven't heard of any other patients having problems with him."

"They most probably haven't lived to tell the tale!"

"Look, let's just see what he says. You can't continue to be in this much pain, it's not right," I plead.

Anne takes a sip of tea. I notice her hand slightly shaking as she lifts the cup to her mouth. It must be the headache, I tell myself. Headaches can make your hand shake.

"OK, Chris," Anne says. "I'll see him."

Five

Dr King

1990

"Mrs Harrison, I can find nothing wrong with you."

Dr King places his stethoscope down on the desk in front of him.

"Well, my balance is off, and my headaches are becoming quite intense," Anne says.

"Take some aspirin, my dear. A lot of housewives come to me with headaches, and often all they need is some aspirin, fresh air and exercise. Fewer glasses of wine whilst their husbands are out at work" – a small laugh – "and the headaches soon resolve." Dr King smiles at Anne and ushers her towards the door.

"Do come back to me if they continue," he adds flippantly, with a wave of his hand.

"I am never going back to that man again, do you hear me, Chris?" Anne sounds furious as she slams her handbag down on the kitchen table.

"Well, what did he say?" I ask.

"He told me to stop drinking wine and to take more aspirin! The cheek. How dare he?" Anne goes upstairs. I hear her drawing the bedroom curtains, then silence. She has gone for another lie down.

I sit at our kitchen table, at a loss as to what to do. There is something wrong with Anne, I know it. I run the list through my mind.

She stumbles in France and from then on loses her balance on several occasions.

Her hands shake.

Her headaches are constant.

The problem with Anne is that she never complains. It is not in her genetic makeup. Nobody in her no-nonsense medical family would ever dream of showing such weakness. If anyone could diagnose what is wrong with Anne, though, it is them. Her father served as a surgeon commander in World War Two and went on to become head of orthopaedics in Bath. Her mother is a qualified chemist, her aunt and numerous cousins are GPs. Added together, they had at least two hundred years' worth of medical experience.

Anne appears at supper time, after her lie down.

"Why don't you speak to your parents about your

headaches?" I ask her tentatively, aware I am edging close to a raw nerve.

"Don't be ridiculous, Chris, what on earth are they going to do? They have enough on their plates without me barking on about some fantasy health concerns. Look, stop worrying. I'm fine."

Predictably, Anne resists going back to the GP. She has lost faith in the system, and just wants to get on with life, headaches or no headaches.

But I can't let it rest.

"Hello? I would like to make an appointment for my wife, Anne Harrison. No, not with Dr King. I think we have reached the end of the road with him. Someone else, please."

A time is arranged for Anne to see a new doctor. This one is more concerned about her symptoms than the dismissive Dr King.

"I suggest you have an MRI scan," Dr Muddiman says earnestly. "Let's see if we can get to the bottom of these headaches. It might take a few weeks. It could be longer. The waiting list is long. At least you are now in the system."

Dr Muddiman smiles at Anne and says the standard parting line.

"Come back to me if your symptoms worsen."

It is six months later that Anne has her MRI brain scan. It's a few days before Christmas, 1992, when we receive the diagnosis.

Six

Diagnosis

1992

"Friedreich's Ataxia."

I repeat the unfamiliar words over and again, like a parrot. I reach for Anne's hand. We are sitting in a bare room at Frenchay Hospital, specialists in patients with brain conditions.

"Yes," the consultant radiologist says. "Friedreich's Ataxia. It's rare. Very rare. It's a genetic disorder, and individuals can only inherit this and develop the disease if *both* parents have the defective gene. Only about ten thousand patients have this diagnosis in the UK."

We sit in silence with this information. What cruel chance.

"Well, is it curable? What can be done about it?" Anne asks, in her usual matter-of-fact, no-nonsense manner.

I'm glad she has asked. I cannot speak. My mind is a jumble of incoherent words and questions.

The consultant hesitates before answering.

"You can expect a slow decline in bodily function. I emphasise the word 'slow'. You might have years before you experience any impairment."

He gives Anne an encouraging smile.

Anne does not smile back.

"I'm sorry, you seem to have misunderstood my question," says Anne, looking the consultant directly in the eye. "What I am asking is this: is this condition life-threatening?"

The consultant sighs and looks back at her.

"You have about ten years before the disease progresses to a stage where you can expect your brain to stop functioning. You are – what, in your early forties? So, yes. I'm sorry to say, your life will be cut short by this disease. I really am very sorry. It will be a long journey – and you will have to be seen by a neurologist throughout that time. To manage your symptoms."

Anne and I sit quietly, processing all these words.

Ten years.

We are handed an information leaflet as we leave, which we take wordlessly.

Ataxia is usually caused by damage to part of the brain known as the cerebellum. It can also be caused by damage to the spinal cord or other nerves. The cerebellum is responsible for:

» *Walking and balance,*
» *Limb co-ordination,*
» *Headaches,*

> » *Uncontrolled or repetitive eye movements,*
> » *Slurred speech,*
> » *Difficulty eating and swallowing.*

The disease does not usually damage the cognitive part of the brain, and there is generally no loss of memory.

"What are you and Louisa going to do?" Anne whispers as we sit beside one another in the car. She is clutching the leaflet tightly, looking out through the front window onto the bleak landscape of the hospital car park.

"What are *we* going to do?" I ask, in surprise.

This was typical of Anne – she gets dealt a devastating blow, her future ripped away, and her first thought is how it will impact us, her beloved husband and daughter.

"We'll get through this," I say hoarsely, gathering her into my arms. "Don't you worry about us. These are only *possible* symptoms. You are strong and healthy in all other ways, I am sure we can beat this together…" I look at her, encouragingly.

Anne laughs dryly and stares at the leaflet in her hand.

"Not a word to anyone," she says, forcefully. She wipes away a tear rolling down her beautiful cheek. "Not my parents, not Louisa. Promise?"

I stare at her. Surely, she isn't asking me to keep a secret of this magnitude all to myself?

"Well… I'm not sure—"

"*Promise* me, Chris."

Anne takes hold of both my arms and glares at me.

"Look," she sighs. "I know it's a lot to ask, and I'm sorry about that. But as the consultant said, it will take years before this disease progresses to a point that I am debilitated by it. There will come a point when it will be impossible to hide my limitations from everyone. We can work out what we are going to say then. But I am not willing to live the rest of my life with pitying gazes following me everywhere I go, do you understand? I want Louisa to have a normal childhood. I don't want this hanging over her, in the way it is going to hang over us. We will manage it by ourselves. Remember what we pledged all those years ago?"

"For better, or worse…" I whisper.

"In sickness and in health…"

Anne kisses me fiercely and sits back, snapping her seat belt on and settling her handbag on her lap. I can see the subject matter is now closed. I put the car into gear and slowly start the drive back home.

Our lives changed forever.

Seven

Altrusa

1990-99

I AM A CAREER MAN, AND I START MY LAST JOB AS director of Western Computers in Bristol in 1990, the year Anne falls ill. For the next two years I juggle everything to try and help her around the home. They always say: 'If you want something done, give it to the busy person.'

That becomes true of me. I keep myself constantly occupied, as a way of coping with the anxiety and sadness of Anne's diagnosis.

In the end it's too much.

I become the Administrator at Bath Abbey. Anne and I throw ourselves into more meaningful altruistic work. It is not lost on us that we have limited time left on earth, all of us. We might as well do good work for others whilst we are here.

Our love of animals results in us becoming more and more involved with Bath Cats and Dogs Home. We immerse ourselves fully in this world. We fundraise, dog walk, and foster dogs and cats. Our house becomes a revolving door for fostered animals, at one point fostering four dogs and three cats, all rescues. Luckily for me, I have found someone else who shares these wide and varied interests, but that is a story for another time.

Anne becomes involved in the more academic side of life. As well as being a Relate counsellor, she takes on the role of chairman of Altrusa, an organisation similar to the Rotary club for women executives and professional leaders as members. She believes passionately in this foundation.

"Anne, do you think you might have enough on your plate already?" I ask, when she first accepts the role. She has recently been diagnosed and I worry she is taking on too much.

"Enough on my plate? Chris, this is a chance for me to do some actual good in the world. Altrusa International Foundation improves everything: economic well-being, quality of life. We need to help the youth where we can, through literacy and encouraging young people to participate in community service. I will not give up on them."

Anne approaches her role in that charity organisation with the same verve and precision she approaches everything in life. She ends up becoming the president for the whole of the south-west, and that is a big deal.

"Wow." I whistle as I skim through the list of the attendants at the next gathering. "Some really big names on here, darling."

"I know, it's great, isn't it?"

"It is," I say proudly. My role is to support her, and that's what I do.

Anne throws herself into helping people in this country and overseas, and engages with everyone with verve and intelligence. She knows exactly how to get what she wants out of people. She has a highly intelligent aura about her, is able to get to know a person intimately and how to use their talents.

At home, she becomes more and more private and closed off. I worry that her diagnosis is playing on her mind, and our communication as a couple stutters to a halt.

Eight

Princess Grace

1962

WE MEET ON A BLIND DATE.

I am living in a bachelor cottage in Devizes, working hard and progressing up the career ladder very satisfactorily.

The phone rings.

"Chris!"

It's Andrew, one of my colleagues from work.

"I'm meeting Susie tonight, at the dance at the town hall. She's bringing a friend. The date we were going to hook her friend up with has just dropped out. Would you like to come along as her chaperone instead?"

I hesitate. Having recently been promoted to director at the wholesale confectioners W H Bourlet, I am feeling tired after a long week at work.

"Oh, why not," I say, making a snap decision. "I quite fancy a dance. Is she pretty?"

"Ha. Just wait until you see her," Andrew says mysteriously, and hangs up.

I see Anne, for the first time, sitting demurely across the room with Andrew's fiancée, Susie. Her blonde hair is beautifully coiffured, she has a trim waist and when she looks up at me as I approach, I see she has a sparkling smile. She looks a picture, like royalty. Like Princess Grace. I can't believe my eyes.

"Excuse me, would you care for this dance?" I enquire, nervously.

Anne smiles up at me and takes my outstretched hand.

"Of course," she says.

We dance all night. I will forever remember the smell of her perfume, the feel of her bare shoulder under my hand.

As we court one another, I fall deeply in love with Anne. She is intelligent, caring and beautiful. Twenty-one years old to my twenty-five. We are in the prime of our lives.

Anne doesn't want to get married at first. She is very careful, meticulous in fact, in the way she has planned out her life. She is going to get her education at the Sorbonne, see the world, not get tied down too quickly. What Anne has not planned for is my determination.

Anne is so beautiful, she has plenty of admirers that I have to get rid of before I stand a chance. One suitor is even in line for becoming the first Sea Lord. I am intimidated at first, but not threatened by such competition. I am going to give it my very best shot.

I woo her day after day, serenading her with renditions of 'Younger than Springtime in the Park'.

And then, eventually, she succumbs.

"How can I resist you, Chris? The singing, the dancing… what a package!"

"I win?" I say, with delight.

"You win. Let's get married."

Nine

Honeymoon

1964

"I THINK I HAVE HAD ENOUGH TIME IN FRANCE, THANK you – may I remind you that I studied at Sorbonne University!" Anne laughs.

We are discussing our forthcoming honeymoon.

"Italy. I always thought we would honeymoon in Italy," I say, looking into her cornflower-blue eyes as she lies on the grass in the park.

"South Africa!" Anne suggests, sitting up with excitement. "We could go and visit your mother. I would love to meet Michael and Aunt Babs. I've heard so much about them…"

I withdraw at the idea of visiting my mother in South Africa. I have a complicated relationship with her, and in particular my stepfather, Tom, whom I have no desire ever to see or hear from again.

"Hardly a relaxing honeymoon destination," I say. "Not with all the politics to contend with."

It is not the right time to start delving into the real reason I don't want to go to South Africa, not when we are both in such a blissfully happy mood. I want to hold on to the romance of our relationship for as long as possible, without tainting it with tales of abandonment and excruciating hurt.

"Ah yes, I suppose with apartheid..." Anne says, knowingly. "All the bloodshed and political uncertainty might put a downer on our trip. You're right, my darling, as always."

Anne twirls a daisy in her fingers.

"Morocco? What do you think? You can remind me of all those wild stories you tell of when you were on the HMS whatever-it-was, during your stint in the navy. Perfect idea. Let's go and relive those battle scenes."

"HMS *New Ark Royal*." I laugh. "Thank you for paying absolutely no attention to anything I tell you."

Anne kisses me in apology, and we lie back, enjoying the warm spring air. Morocco is decided upon, and we plan exotic journeys to Tangiers and Marrakech, all talk of South Africa shelved for another day.

Ten

Louisa Suspects

1999

IT IS 1999.

Louisa, our daughter, takes me to one side.

"Is everything OK at home, Dad?" she asks, her face wrinkled in concern.

"Of course, why wouldn't it be?" I answer.

"I don't know – it's just Mum. She doesn't seem to be getting around easily. Is her back all right? And her hands tremble sometimes too. It's barely there, but it's getting more and more noticeable."

"I'm sure she's fine, Louisa. Walking up and down the hill into Bath is quite taxing on our poor, ancient bodies, you know," I say, laughing, attempting reassurance.

"Yes, I suppose you are both getting quite doddery." Louisa laughs back teasingly.

I protest loudly and theatrically show her my gym-toned arms and calf muscles. The subject is dropped.

"She's starting to ask questions," I say, quietly, to Anne in the kitchen later that afternoon. We are having a family barbecue, and I can hear Anne's mother and Louisa chattering away together outside in the garden.

"Who?" Anne asks, smashing ice cubes into a metal bucket and throwing in a couple of bottles of crisp white wine.

"Louisa!" I hiss. "She has noticed you hobbling a bit, and the shakes in your hand."

Anne picks up a knife and starts slicing cucumber, then puts it down on the chopping board. She drops her head. She has her back to me, and I can't see the expression on her face, so I gently turn her. Tears are brimming in her eyes. She dashes them away with the back of her hand.

"Well, I suppose today is as good as any day to tell them. We can't put it off forever."

And with that, Anne strides out of the kitchen, before I can stop her; do I even want to stop her?

Off to tell our family the awful, life-shattering news.

Eleven

Telling the Family

1999

"FRIEDREICH'S ATAXIA..." I HEAR THE DREADED words floating through the window. I am still standing in the kitchen, unwilling to walk outside and face the music.

I hear Elsie, Anne's mum, sobbing. She knows what it means.

Louisa, frantic: "Why is Grandma crying? Mum? What is it? Why is she crying?"

Anne, matter-of-fact: "I don't have too long left, Louisa. Maybe a few years. Hopefully more."

"It's like motor neurone disease, Louisa," Elsie is explaining, through her sobs.

"But how long have you known?" I hear Louisa say, shell-shocked.

"About seven years. I found out a long time ago. I just didn't want to say. To be treated differently." I can hear Anne's voice shaking with emotion. I want to go out and help her, support her, but I don't want to see the expression on Louisa's face.

Elsie is getting herself under control; the sobs have diminished. I know Elsie will be devastated, having lost her husband, Vernon, and now faced with the reality of losing her only daughter too.

I steady my nerves and walk out into the garden.

I hug Louisa.

"It's all going to be fine. Mummy will be fine. Well, for a while. She's just going to have to take a little more care of herself. We will have to help her out a bit more. OK?"

Louisa looks at me in accusation.

"Why didn't you tell me, Dad? How could you?" Louisa turns and goes and sits in the living room for the rest of the afternoon. Elsie, thank goodness, has pulled herself together and is now asking a hundred medical questions and making plans with Anne about her care.

Inside my heart is breaking, but at least this hurdle is over. I hadn't realised how long I had been dreading this day. One more step towards the real horror of her illness swooping in and taking everything that I know and love about my wife away from me.

Twelve

Adoption

1977

I HAVE NEVER HAD A RELATIONSHIP WITH A WOMAN before Anne. She is my first love in every sense of the word.

Everything is perfect in our lives, except for one area. We are two people in love, but we don't know how to express that love properly.

Years go by, but we are unable to conceive. Her mother had problems. She also found it difficult to fall pregnant, or carry to term, and it appears that Anne has inherited the issue. The longer we try, the more stressful it gets.

"We need to see a doctor," Anne says, after a particularly frustrating month with no sign of the much-longed-for baby.

"More specifically, you have to go and see a doctor. They have done all the tests on me – we know I have a small pelvis, and most possibly a hereditary issue from my mother. But it can't all be down to me," she says. "I've had two D&Cs, tried everything – so, now it's your turn."

I am not keen to go and get tested, but, Anne is right, it is only fair.

"Well, Mr Harrison," says the doctor. "Your sperm count is low. That might explain some of the difficulty you and Anne are having, conceiving."

"Why? What causes that? Can it be fixed?" I am horrified.

So, it's me. And all this time we had thought the problem was with Anne. This is difficult to get my head around.

"It could be because of your childhood mumps. It sounds like you had a very severe case, and it is a known cause for low sperm count," the doctor explains.

"Well, what do you suggest?" I ask.

"Here is a prescription for injections to increase sperm motility and count," the doctor says, scribbling furiously on his pad. "I'm not going to lie to you. The injections will be most unpleasant. So. See how it goes."

It does not go well. The doctor is right. The injections are painful, but worse than that, it turns out they are ineffective.

By this point Anne has psychologically associated our attempts at love-making with pain and loss, so our instances of being intimate with each other become fewer and further apart as the months go on. I am desperate to show her love, but she is both physically and emotionally closed off from me. It feels like an unspoken curse in our relationship. Looking back, it is a blessing from God in disguise, as we will see.

Luckily, I have my religion and moral compass to keep me on the straight and narrow – the idea of straying from Anne to fall into the arms of another woman never once crosses my mind. By my late thirties, early forties, it has become clear that trying for, or indeed, conceiving a baby, is not going to come naturally to us. It is a terrible blow to our relationship.

"We need to start the adoption process, now, Chris, before it gets too late," Anne pleads.

"OK, my love. Let's do it."

I would be lying if I told you I was not nervous. I knew it would be a brutal process.

Adoption, and dealing with social services, is a real eye-opener. We are subjected to in-depth scrutiny in all areas of our life. Ladies in tweed skirts with numerous clipboards and files visit us at home to check our suitability and to puzzle the pieces together to form the right match. They ask us probing private and personal questions, to decide among themselves whether we are committed to maintaining a solid marriage and staying together. It is strange how much anxiety this creates for us. Of course, we are committed. We love each other. But, admittedly, over the past few years we have started to bicker. This is what inability to conceive does to relationships. We are terrified of them finding out about our little squabbles.

Private to a fault, especially Anne, we hate finding ourselves in the position of having to answer intimate questions about our relationship and lifestyle to complete strangers. A process that lasts for two years.

"It's so intrusive, Anne. Are you sure you want to keep going with this?" I ask more than once.

"Absolutely, Chris, it will be worth it," Anne always replies. And as always, she is right.

Our new daughter, Louisa, comes to live with us when she is six weeks old. From the day we carry her home, it is like it is meant to be. Very quickly I find myself loving Louisa as much as if I had given birth to her myself.

Anne's love for her is just as strong, and it is a real privilege to watch the relationship between mother and daughter grow.

In the future, Louisa will become a mother herself, to three children. Our beautiful grandchildren.

Sadly my Anne will never live to see the day.

Thirteen

Mangar

2000

SO FAR, I HAVE TALKED ABOUT ANNE IN TERMS OF OUR lives together, but not about what she was truly like: as a person, as a wife, as a patient. Let me try and explain.

Anne has an enigmatic personality. She is humble, warm and friendly to strangers and acquaintances, but hers is a much harder exterior when it comes to dealing with the people closest to her. Anne is blessed with a great bedside manner. She has, after all, grown up in a medical family. Everyone loves the 'Grace Kelly of Bath' – my very own Princess Grace. As well as her kind and loving nature, Anne is so striking that fashion model scouts stop her in the street to ask if she would be willing to wear the latest Hartnell designs.

Anne endears herself to everyone she meets.

After the adoption of Louisa, Anne trains to become a

careers advisor. She helps in a specialist school for children with various learning difficulties. This is her passion, not strutting down the runway as a model. Her empathy and dedication to helping others also sees her volunteering as a Relate counsellor.

As you can see, Anne is kind to a fault. She selflessly helps anyone who needs her.

But she is also organised and stubborn.

"You are too assertive, Anne," I say, as she takes control of everything, including my career path.

"Nonsense, Chris. What would you do without me? I'm the mother you always needed, you always say that."

This is indeed true. She has slotted very neatly into the large mother-shaped void in my world. This makes the next section of my life very difficult to bear.

I lose both my real mother, and my substitute one.

Anne's stubborn character trait becomes more and more evident as the years of illness go by, and the Friedreich's Ataxia symptoms worsen. Anne has to relinquish her motherly control and has to learn to rely on me instead. It is a hard adjustment for both of us.

Anne holds the opinion that she is the carer, and not the one to be cared for. This suited me in the early years of married life, when I craved the compassion and control of a motherly figure, having had that denied to me as a youngster. As her disease progresses, though, it becomes clear that the roles are starting to switch.

"Don't make a fuss, Chris," becomes her standard

retort. I do make a fuss. I can't help it. I don't want her to suffer.

As time goes on, her frustration at having to rely on me and others becomes more pronounced.

"You're just a big bully," Anne screams at me one awful, memorable day.

She has fallen, and is lying on the living room floor, twisted limbs like a discarded rag doll. I am wrestling with a Mangar, a rubber inflatable medical contraption. She is being particularly resistant to allowing me to slide it underneath her, but I need to, so that I can inflate it and get her up off the floor more easily. She cannot lift herself up unaided, and my knees and shoulder are injured and too bad to haul her up myself.

I am shocked. I never thought of myself as a bully.

"Anne, darling. You're just upset," I say, tentatively.

"No. I'm not. You're a bully. I don't even want to look at you. Leave me."

A single tear rolls down her cheek.

I can't leave her there on the floor, of course, and she knows this.

I bend down again, wincing at the pain in my own knee, and manage to roll her onto the Mangar. I pump it up to the point that I am able to pull her up by her elbow. Once on her feet, she grabs on to the back of the armchair and looks at me. I manage to get myself up, and bend at the waist, gasping.

Anne has begun falling more and more frequently. It is

so much effort getting her back up to standing. In these moments, I feel so totally and completely alone. There is no one to help. Just me, the hated Mangar and my dying wife.

She rages.

"A bully, Chris. You are!"

"Why? Why do you keep saying these hurtful things to me?" I feel tears forming. This is not the kind Anne I have known all these years. The disease is taking away more than her ability to move. I am beginning to think the frustration of her illness is starting to affect her personality.

"You know why. Constantly asking me to go to this physio and that nurse, and this occupational therapist. I am managing perfectly well, I don't need you to arrange things. You are trying to control me!"

"You know why I have to, Anne! You are so stubborn. Look at the effort I had to put in, just to get you to accept having the MRI. Your symptoms are getting worse. Every week I notice a new change in you. You might not, but I do!"

I don't usually speak back to Anne when she is in one of these moods, but I can't hold back this time.

Anne gives a big sigh and half-falls into the armchair in front of her.

"I know this must be hard for you," she starts, more gently. "But it's *my* disease, it's *my* body and it's *my* life. I don't want a nurse to come and help around the house. You know I am a very private person. I would find it too intrusive."

"I can't cope," I say, quietly.

"Sorry?"

"Anne, I'm the one that's sorry," I say more firmly. "I can't cope with this anymore. I am alone. Our friends have abandoned us. My body is a wreck. My knee is giving way, my shoulder ligaments are torn. I have to carry you from room to room, shuffling you wherever you want to go. We need to talk seriously about getting you a wheelchair. And a nurse to come in more regularly to help out. I can't do it myself anymore."

Anne stares at me, her expression a mix of softness and stone.

"Leave me, Chris," she repeats. I go next door to the kitchen and make us both a cup of tea.

Another day, another battle.

Fourteen

Supermarket

2001

"CHRIS! ANNE – HOW ARE YOU?" SANDRA COMES OVER to us in the supermarket, with a huge smile. "We haven't seen you for ages. How are things?"

I feel Anne tighten her grip on my arm, and she leans more heavily into me.

"Good, good!" I reply, grasping at Anne's waist to keep her upright.

"Anne, are you coming to the fundraiser next week? I know you've been laying low recently, but the other ladies would love to catch up?"

"I... I'm not feeling very well at the moment. If I feel up to it, I would love to come. Maybe you could drop in for a cup of tea one day?"

Anne's speech is slurred, and she has difficulty getting the words out.

I have become used to Anne talking this way, but

Sandra looks shocked. I suddenly realise. It is a very long time since we have seen any of our friends.

"Sorry? What did you say?" Sandra asks, alarm on her face.

"Anne's not feeling great at the moment," I answer, stepping in. "But do stop by one day? I know she would appreciate the visit, wouldn't you, Anne?"

Anne nods.

I smile back at Sandra.

She looks confused.

"Has she… has she had a stroke?" she asks me, as if Anne is not there.

There is nothing wrong with Anne's cognitive abilities. Inside, she is as bright, clever and alert as she has always been.

"No, I haven't," Anne says, slowly and quite clearly.

"Anne has a condition that affects her muscles, that's all. Some days are worse than others. We just take things a bit slower now," I explain.

"Oh. OK. Well, lovely to see you, Anne," Sandra says, raising her voice, as if Anne's malfunctioning muscles are having a direct effect on her hearing.

We begin turning down invitations, stop going out, avoid social contact, and as a consequence, our friends start dropping off the scene, one by one. Ours had been a very active social life, before. We used to go to dances, concerts, fundraisers for Bath Abbey and the Cats and Dogs Trust, where we were both volunteers.

I suppose it is good our friends are out of touch. They

do not want to see Anne in her slow decline. I find it difficult enough myself.

But we are isolated. Particularly Anne.

I still go to the gym at the Royal Bath Spa. This is a routine I don't deviate from. It is the one hour when I can focus completely on myself and release all my worries. It is imperative I keep myself fit, to handle the increasingly physical demands that Anne's illness is putting on me.

There is still one friend. The one friend Anne can confide in and rely on. She has stuck by us through thick and thin, and I do not know how I could cope without her.

Fifteen

Deidre Offers to Take the Dogs

2000

DEIDRE (DEE) IS THE BEST FRIEND THAT ANNE COULD ever have, and a godsend to me too. They met at the careers advisor office in Bristol where they both worked, and quickly became firm pals. Dee has a forthright and kind manner, meaning she can talk sense into Anne when Anne is in one of her obstructive moods. She is able to explain things far more clearly than I can. I seem to spend much time in a state of bewilderment these days. Deidre keeps me sane. She understands Anne and her need for privacy. Dee also understands me, and what I am going through. She shares my love for Anne, as well as the frustrations, and is the only person I can talk to in our increasingly isolated world.

When our home becomes our private nursing home, life changes dramatically for both of us. Anne continues to fight her illness with determination and strength. She throws all her energy into her first love, looking after the three rescued cats and four rescued dogs from the home. Anne and I had been trustees for the Bath Cats and Dogs Home for the past twenty years. As General Manager of the home, I had personally overseen the rebuilding of kennels, offices, and vets' facilities, costing over £1.5 million, so was very much involved myself. We were the only animal home in the country to have a non-destruction policy and would only ever euthanise dangerous animals. Anne found it very difficult not to want to rehome all of them.

Dee is over for tea. She visits often, and I look forward to hearing her cheerful voice calling out as she comes to the front door.

She fondles the soft ear of our rescue beagle.

"This poor little fellow. What will become of him when Anne passes?"

I look at the lovely dog.

"I know," I say sadly. "He's already suffered enough in his life. Used for research on the effects of smoking in humans. Imagine?"

Anne was particularly passionate about beagles, and we had rescued over forty beagles in our time at the home with the help of the RSPCA.

Dee looks over at our other rescues, a collie cross, a feisty Fox Terrier and a Yorkie named Penny, who never left Anne's side.

"I think these animals keep Anne going," Dee says. "I really do. When she dies, Chris, I think it's going to be hard for you to handle them. I will have them, if that would help."

I am speechless with gratitude. I know that I won't be able to manage them when Anne goes. I nod and thank God again for the presence of Dee in our lives.

Deidre is a friend to everybody, no sides to her whatsoever. Her ability to listen and empathise, and not judge, makes her invaluable to me and to Anne.

She is an amazing person, and someone I always include in my prayers.

Sixteen

Cheated and Dee

2001

"I've been cheated," Anne sobs.

"What do you mean?" I say, concerned. I am sitting beside Anne on the bed. "Who has cheated you?"

"We're in the middle of what's supposed to be the best time of our life and look, it's all been taken away from us. You have suffered so much hardship already, with the trauma of your childhood, and now you are suffering all over again."

This outburst was very unlike Anne. She was not prone to self-pity. In fact, her caring nature meant that she was easily able to deflect any conversation about her personal feelings. I envied her that.

"What can I do, Anne?" I ask, distressed at seeing her show her vulnerable side. Anne is always the strong one.

"I need to see Deidre," she says. "Dee will sort me out."

"Why can't I help?" I ask, hurt.

"I feel too guilty talking to you about this. I'm sorry."

I feel sorry too. It seems we have moved into a new phase, and I am now unable to help my beloved wife in her darkest times. It's upsetting. I feel redundant.

"It's OK," I say, pushing my feelings aside. I have to. I'm not the one dying. "I will see what I can do."

I call Deidre. She comes over as soon as she can get away.

"Hello, Deidre, my love," Anne says, as we both enter her bedroom. I walk over and take her hand. She turns her head to me. "Thank you," she whispers. I lean over and give her a kiss on her head.

"Chris tells me you have got yourself in a bit of a state," Dee says, bustling around to the other side of Anne's bed. She pushes Anne's little dog Penny over and sits down on the duvet.

"This isn't like you, my darling. Tell me what's up."

"I'll leave you to it," I whisper, and back out of the room, closing the bedroom door.

Deidre walks into the kitchen and I hand her a cup of tea.

"She's having a rest now," Dee says. "She's very emotional and tired today. I've never seen her like this."

"Neither have I," I admit. "It's worrying, isn't it?"

Deidre sips her tea.

"Talking of worry – she's worried about you."

"I know she is, but why?" I ask.

"'He's not going to be good on his own,'" Dee says. "That's what she told me."

I think about this. Anne's correct. I'm not going to be good on my own. I function, thrive even, because I have Anne alongside me, making decisions, using her calm logic and her strength of character to guide us through our lives. All those years ago, Anne had stepped in and rescued me. Anne's illness means the inevitable. I am going to be abandoned all over again.

What on earth would I do when she wasn't there anymore? I could barely think about it.

"Don't stress," Deidre says, smiling at me gently and taking my hand in hers. "I will be here. I will always be here for both of you. Whatever you need."

I smile at her, truly grateful.

"I think you're an Angel sent from Heaven, Deidre," I say. "Whatever would we do without you?"

Seventeen

Apartheid

1967

"WE MUST VISIT HER," I SAY, CLATTERING ABOUT IN the kitchen. I am doing the washing up.

"Why, Chris? What has your mother ever done for you? Apart from make you deeply miserable, and cause you some deep-seated emotional issues?" Anne says, direct and to the point as ever. She is sweeping the terracotta floor, briskly. The noise is starting to get on my nerves.

I stop scrubbing and squeeze the water out the green abrasive sponge. I carefully place the large platter that had held the roast chicken down on the draining board and wipe my foamy hands on the good white tea towel with the flowery embroidery.

"I just think that it would be good for me. Please, Anne, indulge me. I have such happy childhood memories. I was going to move back to South Africa after my apprenticeship at Sharps, remember? Due to… various things happening, I wasn't able to. I think now is the time," I say, carefully.

"Various things happening? Meaning… marrying me?" Anne says.

"Err, yes, but also the company takeovers and general career trajectory. Come on, let's go. It's only for a little holiday," I plead. "Mum wasn't able to make it to our wedding, and I would love to introduce you. You wanted to go for our honeymoon, remember?"

"Fine. We will go, if it's that important to you. I'm just very reluctant to visit South Africa right now, because of the political environment. A concern you rightly pointed out during our discussions about our honeymoon, if you remember!"

"Well, not much we can do about apartheid now. Just try and ignore it," I say, picking up the telephone to call the travel agent.

Finally, I am heading home.

Anne is silent as we drive through Cape Town towards Hermanus. Over-excited on the flight over from London, I barely notice how quiet she is. I introduce Anne to everyone, and even my mother, who can be a difficult woman, is charmed. I am happy to have Anne with me, so I can ease myself back into forming a new relationship with my mother via her. My mother hurt me deeply, and I am wary around her, but Anne doesn't have that history. Thankfully, Anne also gets on famously with my cousins and other relatives, with whom I have always maintained great relationships.

They were a large part of my very happy childhood, before I was sent away.

I am in my element, greedily exploring all the areas of my youth. I take Anne whale-watching from clifftops, I threaten her with trips to swim with great white sharks, I whirl with childish glee on Muizenberg Beach. All I want is for my beloved Anne to love South Africa as much as I do.

She doesn't.

"Come on, Anne, cheer up!" I say one day, as we walk hand in hand through the Fernkloof Nature reserve. There is lush vegetation as far as the eye can see, and I breathe in the coastal air with delight. I am transported time and time again to my childhood and happier times. Anne sadly doesn't experience the same pull.

"I just can't enjoy it here, Chris. You tell me to ignore apartheid, but how can I? How can *you*? This political system still in place, of a white minority rule sanctioning racial, political and economic segregation against non-whites… it's appalling."

Anne is so angry, her pale face is flushing.

"Aren't you enjoying meeting my family? Seeing the beautiful scenery?" I ask, trying to move her away from the subject of apartheid.

"Scenery? How can you talk about scenery? Yesterday, when you took me to the beach. Blacks this side, whites there. Wrong! On buses, trains, in hotels, and restaurants! It's all so wrong! How can this still be going on in this day and age? When we drove through the shanty towns around the Cape flats… I felt sick to my stomach. I cannot enjoy my time here, with my privilege, when all around me I see poverty and squalor. I cannot wait to get to Kenya. That's all I'm saying on the matter."

We book flights to Kenya soon after this conversation, curtailing my time in Hermanus. My enjoyment of my childhood home is tainted by Anne's strong reaction against it.

Luckily, Kenya is a different experience altogether. We travel to Mombasa, then on to the Serengeti Natural Game Reserve. Anne visibly relaxes, thrilled with the experience and all the wildlife. She returns to her cheerful normal self.

We are enjoying post-safari cocktails in the glow of the setting sun, basking in the memory of having seen the big five that day.

"Extraordinary day," Anne sighs contentedly, sipping her cold drink.

"I can't believe we spotted that magnificent white rhino. They say the rhino might die out in the next thirty years or so, because of the poachers," I say. "I feel blessed to have seen it."

"Yes. We really are blessed. Humans are horrid." Anne leans forward, suddenly alert, and pushes her large dark sunglasses on top of her head. She points. "Look! Look over there! Is that a family of hogs walking down to the watering hole? Look how sweet the tiny ones are! Oh, Chris. Now this is what I call heaven," Anne says, picking up her binoculars and peering through them at the truffling animals in the distance.

"I'm glad to see you're back to your old self," I say, cautiously, taking the offered pair of binoculars and searching out the hogs in the gloom of the approaching dusk.

"I am surprised at you! How can you not hate it all?" Anne says firmly back. "I absolutely detest the shallow lives of all those entitled white South Africans. All those ridiculous bridge parties, playing golf all the time and drinking too much."

Anne takes a long, thirsty sip of her G&T.

I raise my eyebrow and wordlessly point at the drink in her hand.

"This is different, Chris, and you know it," Anne says, defensively. "You know I've always enjoyed the finer things in life. The difference is, I don't knowingly exploit other people when doing so!"

She takes another long sip and raises her glass in cheers. We clink, both laugh and sit back to enjoy the wildlife show.

Eighteen

Buying Alpine Cottage

1977

On the flight back from Nairobi, I know that Anne and I will never visit South Africa together again. Luckily we have so much else to occupy our full lives together. So I am able to push away the awful thought that I will never return to my spiritual home with my beloved wife.

The idea of returning to South Africa is quashed until after Anne dies. Then it comes back with a vengeance.

We adopt Louisa ten years after our trip to Africa. Ten long years of trying for a child, which brings its own trials and tribulations. To fill our time during those ten years, we work, go to the theatre, enjoy exhibitions. We particularly love the Impressionists and travel to London often to visit the galleries. Music stays a constant, as does dancing. Until Anne can't dance anymore, that is. We take up gardening and explore our love for animals. All connecting interests that bring us much joy during trying times.

To everyone's shock, Anne's dad dies suddenly just after we adopt Louisa, and that causes much upheaval.

"Let's buy Alpine Cottage," Anne says.

"Alpine Cottage?" I ask, in surprise.

"Yes. I can't bear to not live there, Chris. I spent most of my childhood in that house. So many of my great memories come from living in Alpine Cottage. Let's make some of our own, especially now we have Louisa."

"But where will your mother live?" I ask.

"We need to think about that," Anne says, stubbornly. I look at her. I am suspicious of her tone. There is no way I am living with Anne's mother, however wonderful she is. Anne's mother, whom I have always admired with her strength, has started to crumble under the weight of her grief after Vernon died. She has started relying on Anne more and more as an emotional crutch, and I am not sure I want to share my marriage and my home with my mother-in-law.

After much discussion and negotiation, we sell our small house in Bradford-on-Avon and move into Alpine Cottage. There is a small, complicated crossover, where I experience what it's like to live with a grieving mother-in-law and a small baby, but thankfully, we manage to find Elsie a house a hundred yards from us. Near enough for Anne to feel comfortable, and far enough away for me to retain my sanity. Anne juggles her mother, new-born Louisa, her career and me.

It all works out in the end. Just another dip in our very bumpy journey through life.

Nineteen

Anne's Mother

1978

ANNE IS AN ONLY CHILD. WHEN HER FATHER DIES SO early on in our relationship, her mother Elsie becomes very reliant on her. It is an interesting study for me, how different people cope with grief. Anne's mother is a very self-sufficient and qualified person, but she needs so much love and friendship from her daughter to survive. That's how Anne's mum Elsie copes, how she gets through each day: by clinging on to Anne. After Anne's diagnosis, and seeing Elsie's reliance on Anne first-hand, I often wonder how alone and needy I will feel when she dies.

I make a vow to myself.

However alone I feel, I don't ever want to burden Louisa in the same way.

We buy the house down the road for Elsie and move out of our little house in Bradford-on-Avon. We have some renovations done on Alpine Cottage which takes longer to get ready than expected, and we end up having to live with her.

We share a bedroom, cooking and living on top of each other. Louisa is now on the scene as well. It gets a little crowded, especially with a new baby. Six months of living like this, it gets quite traumatic. I admit I do not cope with it very well. I feel myself become distant from Anne, which in turn pushes her closer to her mother.

"Chris, we should take Mum," Anne says one day.

"Where?" I ask idly, tinkering with the underside of my beloved Morris van. "Pass me the wrench, will you?"

"To Europe. This summer."

I scoot out from under the car and sit up.

"On our summer holiday? Anne, really?" I say, hating myself for my ungenerous tone.

This is Anne's newly widowed mother, but we are a married couple with a new baby. The idea of having to take Anne's mum away with us for weeks on end on our annual holiday, as well as having endured the past six months living with her, makes my heart sink.

"Let's say it's non-negotiable, Chris. I travelled with you when you wanted to visit your mother in South Africa," Anne retorts, and goes back into the house. "Against my wishes, I might add…" her voice floats out through the open door.

I sigh and lie back down on the ground, wrench in hand.

We take Anne's mother to Europe that year, and then for many years after that. We tour all over. We travel at a time in history when it's quite easy to jump in a car and off you go, wherever you want.

"Let's fly," I suggest one time, the idea of driving thousands of miles making me feel exhausted just thinking about it.

"You know I can't fly, Chris. I only have one lung. I would die up there, in the plane. From the lack of the oxygen, you see," Anne's mum exclaims in panic.

"Don't mind me, I'm just your resident Thomas Cook Tour Operator, taxi at your service," I grumble mildly. It's a joke I repeat many times over the years. It never fails to make everyone laugh.

So drive we must, on our great European adventures, all squeezed into my little car.

To be honest, I don't mind so much. We do everything together. We visit countless art galleries, theatres, museums. Cultural activities we all enjoy. One memorable year, Anne and I book to see a magnificent Tutankhamen Exhibition in Paris. We feel special, lucky to see it and become a part of history – that particular exhibition set a visitor attendance record that still stands to this day.

One year, even Anne's Aunt Madeleine travels with us on our annual holiday, all of us bundled up, chugging all the way to Italy in my little car. She is a lovely woman, Madeleine. Disabled, yet strong-willed and full of energy. Undeterred by her disability, she is a proud Welsh woman and works in Cardiff. Despite her relative independence, I am always on guard, always on duty; looking out for both

Elsie and Madeleine. It isn't a very relaxing time of my life and I am often bone-tired.

"Anne, I don't feel we ever get the chance to talk, you know? Get to really know each other? I feel we might be drifting apart," I say one day during a rare walk down by the olive groves without being accompanied by her mother or aunt.

"What? Don't be silly, Chris. We've been married a few years now. Of course we know each other."

And that is the end of the conversation. Private to the core, Anne never lets anything slip.

I only realise how odd this is when I have a more open relationship in the future with Pauline.

Twenty

Anne's Mother Gets Ill

2001

"I HAVE BOWEL CANCER."

"What? No!" Anne gasps.

Her mother Elsie puts her hand over her daughter's hand. I notice Anne's hand shaking with shock on top of the usual tremor.

"I'm sorry, dear. You have enough to deal with, without all this."

"What can they do about it? What are the next steps?" Anne asks, tearfully.

"I will have treatment at the local hospital. It's just a bus ride away from me."

"Don't worry, Chris will take you," Anne volunteers immediately.

"Of course I will," I reassure them both.

Inwardly, my heart sinks. Anne's illness is progressing rapidly, and life is complicated enough attending to her needs without having to take on the care of her mother. Hopefully Elsie's treatment will prove quick and effective, and everything can go back to normal.

Life doesn't go back to normal. It is up to me to organise taking both Anne and her mother everywhere. I shuttle them where they need to go, whether it's to the supermarket, to physio, or to the frequent doctor appointments. Anne's mother has the same stoic attitude as Anne and is very resistant to having a colostomy bag after her bowel operation, so there is much discussion about that. My shoulders ache from lifting them both out of the car. How long can I keep doing this?

As it turns out, not that long at all, sadly.

Anne and I privately discuss the option of placing Anne's mother, an elderly woman in her eighties, in the geriatric ward of St Martin's Hospital.

"She can't go in there, Chris, she will never recover! She's a proud Welsh woman, she will hate it!" Anne says, voice slurring, tapping her hand against her leg in frozen agitation.

"Well, what do you want me to do, Anne? As much as I would like to, I can't look after you both!" I reply.

I am suffering physically a lot by this point, particularly with carrying both of them around. Anne is in a wheelchair by now, a decision that creates a lot of resistance on her part. Another fight of the many that are now part of daily life.

I think back to the argument Dee and I had with Anne, trying to get her to accept the chair.

"Anne, you can't keep doing this," Deidre states, matter-of-fact, after Anne suffers a particularly brutal fall. Anne won't listen to me, so I have called Dee in to help.

"I don't want to lose my freedom," Anne explains.

"This will give you more freedom," Dee replies. "Don't you agree?"

Anne finally sees sense and accepts that the wheelchair is now going to be part of her future, another sacrifice to normal life.

Twenty-One

My Health

2001

ANNE'S HEALTH DETERIORATING BEFORE MY EYES AND the extra hours put in for caring for Anne's mother has, I am horrified to discover, taken its toll on my once fit and healthy body.

"I'm seizing up!" I laugh, coming to the end of one particularly gruelling day of pain. I flop down on the sofa next to Dee and stretch out my leg in front of me, trying to ease the agony.

We have started to adapt the house to Anne's changing needs; a helpful improvement. Still, it's hard on my knees and shoulders, hauling Anne into and out of the hoists, getting her in and out of the wheelchair in order to push her down into town to do the shopping.

"Not you too, Chris! Well, get yourself checked out quickly, for God's sake," Dee says to me, patting my knee gently. She keeps a watchful eye over me as I hobble around after a day of hard physical work caring for Anne and tries to remove the burden off me as much as possible.

"You need surgery to repair the ligaments and rotator cuffs on both your shoulders," says the doctor.

More bad news delivered at a time that I really need to hear something positive.

I also need two procedures on ulcerated legs, and a major operation to remove my sigmoid colon and large section of my bowel. As Anne deteriorates further, I too am having to deal with health problems of my own. I am disorientated and confused a lot of the time, dosed to the hilt on a high cocktail of drugs, including morphine, to relieve the pain.

"We need a nurse, Anne," I say, one day, having waited for the right moment.

"I don't want someone in my house," Anne states, in her usual stubborn way.

"But look at me." I wave my hand down my body. "I'm sixty, I've had to give up work to care for you full-time, and it's still not enough. I need another pair of hands, particularly on tough days like this when I can barely move myself."

Anne is, in all ways, a kind soul. She is able to put her own misgivings aside when she realises what I am having to endure.

"OK, Chris. I'm sorry. I didn't realise how bad you were feeling. You're right, you need a bit of a break."

Anne smiles at me.

Another day, another battle won.

Twenty-Two

Anne's Mother Dies

1st April 2002

Elsie is placed in the 'care of the elderly' ward when she can't cope with her colostomy bag. This is not a good time for anyone.

"I want to visit her," Anne whispers.

"Are you sure, Anne? You aren't the strongest yourself at the moment."

"I need to, Chris. I can't bear the idea of her being in there all alone with no one there to talk to her." Anne looks upset, and I wonder if she is thinking about her own mortality. We never talk about it. It's one of our 'off-limits' topics. Death can never be discussed without her shutting the conversation down immediately.

We arrive at St Martin's and head up to the geriatric ward. The pungent smell of urine and the unpleasant odour of an unconnected stoma bag fills the air. I try not to gag as

I wheel Anne down the ward. I wonder how the patients themselves could stand it, and then remember that often older people lose their sense of smell and are unaware of their surroundings. The ward is full, with about fourteen or fifteen beds occupied. I am surprised to see that they have mixed up both male and female patients, and worry about privacy. The lack of dignity for these poor souls at the end of their long and noble lives makes me sad. Some, thankfully, have curtains around their bed, so they have a modicum of privacy at least. The flip side to that would be their isolation. I try not to think about that.

"Good morning, Elsie!" I say brightly, wheeling Anne next to the bed so that Elsie can see her face.

"Is it?" Elsie grumbles, weakly.

"Oh, Mum, what's the matter?" Anne says, slurring.

"What did she say?" Elsie says, turning to me.

Anne always tries to engage her mother in conversation on our visits, but Elsie's hearing is not good, and the combination of that with Anne's slurred speech makes it difficult for them to understand each other. I am there to fulfil the role of translator.

"She asked what's the matter, Elsie," I say, loudly.

"Another bad night, that's all," Elsie says. "It's impossible to sleep with the snoring and whimpering of all these oldies." Elsie waves her gnarled hands at the ward. I look around to see if anyone has noticed her rudeness. No one bats an eyelid.

"Always crying out for the nurses, they are," Elsie says.

"Well, you take up a lot of their time," says a bright-eyed old man from across the way. He is reading a newspaper, which rustles loudly with the tremor in his hand.

Elsie looks startled at the sound of the man's voice.

"Vernon? Where's Vernon?" Elsie asks, suddenly agitated.

Anne looks at her, then turns to me with sadness in her eyes.

I sit next to Elsie on the bed and take her hand.

"Vernon is dead, Elsie, remember?" I say, gently.

Elsie purses her mouth and turns her head to Anne. She stares at her silently for a minute.

"Why is she in that chair?"

Anne says nothing.

"Is she going to die?" Elsie asks, still looking at Anne.

"Well, Elsie, we are all going to die," I say, trying to make a light joke.

"Hmm. She looks like she's fading. What's wrong with her face?" Elsie continues to stare at Anne. Suddenly her face crumples in on itself. "I remember. No recovery. Not ever."

Elsie starts to cry, and I hand her a tissue. Anne is trying not to look distressed, but I know this will be very difficult for her.

"I just want out," Elsie moans, closing her eyes.

"Out?" I ask.

"Out of life. I'm so tired. She's probably going to die before I do. What's the point of living?"

Elsie points at Anne and looks up at me.

"I won't cope, when she goes. My darling, my Anne… I can't take it," Elsie wails.

I can see Anne is getting more and more upset.

"Elsie, we have to go now," I say, loudly. "We will see you on Tuesday."

We leave Elsie weeping, all the other patients ignoring her.

We continue to visit Anne's mother three or four times a week. It is very upsetting to see someone who has been so active all her life, a highly articulate and well-educated person like Elsie, slip into a state of oblivion.

"She's like a lost soul, Chris, with no will to live," Anne slurs. "I hate it. I hate seeing her battle with her stoma. I don't want to see all that, Chris."

"What are the options, Anne? We could stop visiting her, but I don't think that would make you any happier," I suggest.

Anne is quiet, the hopelessness of the situation clear in her eyes.

We continue to visit, and our visits last over two hours sometimes, until the uninspiring evening meal would arrive. Anne finds it exhausting, but she never complains.

"Maybe we don't have to go so often," I say one day, horrified to discover how bad Anne's pressure sores are from sitting in her wheelchair after the long visits.

"That is absolutely not an option, Chris. Just get me more of those special cushions. You know, to prevent the sores. I will keep going as long as it takes."

As long as it takes. This was Anne all over, determined in the face of pain and adversity to the last.

I pass the time on our visits by attempting to talk to the other patients. It is a bit of a hit-and-miss affair, trying to find the ones who don't have dementia or Alzheimer's.

When I find the ones on the ward dying from old age, but perfectly lucid, it is particularly rewarding for me. I have lots of interesting chats and learn a lot from them. They are the good times.

Just to think, in less than a year, both Anne and her mother would be dead.

Anne's mother dies on the 1st of April, 2002.

Some April Fool.

Anne is devastated.

Her grief is hard for her to deal with. I wonder if she is suffering the double effect of reliving the grief of the early death of her father at sixty to cancer. At the time, Anne managed his death in the same way she dealt with everything: matter-of-fact, with minimal fuss. The death of her mother, however, knocks her sideways.

"I'm an orphan now, Chris," she says to me one day, tears sliding down her cheeks.

Twenty-Three

Power of Attorney
Legal Battle

2002

THIS IS THE START OF ONE OF THE WORST YEARS OF MY life. Before Elsie dies, I am granted power of attorney for Anne's mother, and am responsible for her welfare in every respect. Getting her into hospital, finding a nursing home, arranging her funeral. When Elsie dies, it is also my responsibility to clear her house and sell it.

"Anne, I think I have no choice. I think we have to sue your mother's solicitor," I say to Anne one day.

"Why?" Anne asks, in alarm. Her grief and her illness have worsened daily since her mother's death, so this is the first time I have spoken to her about the subject. I have tried my best to shield her from the complications arising from the legal case I have been embroiled in since that day. Elsie's solicitor, a person she had trusted for many years, had been instructed by

Anne's mother to set up a trust for Anne. It has gone very badly.

"Well, you know how your mother had wanted to set up a trust for you? It now transpires that they were negligent in the way that they did that. They have dealt with it most unprofessionally. It means your mother's estate has suffered an increased liability of £30,000 estate duty."

"Oh, Chris, I don't care about the money," Anne says, turning her head away from me.

I am also past caring about the money, but I haven't worked for several years because of having to take care of Anne full-time, and her equipment and care is close to bankrupting us. That £30,000 from her mother's estate is due to her and would help in making the final years of her life more comfortable.

So I carry the burden alone, battling the solicitor's firm, with no one to talk to about the stress and additional admin I find myself having to undertake.

The solicitor's firm finally admit negligence and settle out of court, paying full costs.

Just as they settle, and I feel an enormous burden is lifted, my beloved Anne dies.

Twenty-Four

I Owe You

Spring 2002

"I AM SO THANKFUL FOR EVERYTHING YOU ARE DOING," Anne says to me one day.

I look up from unloading the shopping from the boot of the car. I am surprised. It must have been hard for Anne to say this. It is a sign of her accepting defeat.

"I owe you, Anne. I owe everything to you. I could care for you until the end of time," I say. "And it would still never pay back what you have done for me."

"Don't be silly." Anne laughs.

"You are the only person in the world who understands me," I say, placing the shopping bags on the ground and placing my hand on Anne's arm. "Do you know what that means? You, and only you, turned my life around, gave me a loving home, for the first time in my life, and kept me on the straight and narrow. I could never repay you, not in a million years."

It is true, Anne sees my weakness, my vulnerability – when we first met, and now. She understands the impact of being abandoned by my mother all those years ago, and the effect it had on my feelings of self-worth.

"I guess my experience as a Relate counsellor has been helpful over the years. But it doesn't mean that you owe me," Anne says.

"Yes, it does! Your compassion saved me when I was adrift. You guided me through the suffering I went through with the emotional loss of my mother. You put up with me when I was truly hell to live with."

Anne squeezes my hand.

"It was my pleasure. Remember, Chris. You are stronger than you think," she says.

In the not-too-distant future, I will think back on her words. There are many moments I don't feel strong in any way.

Twenty-Five

District Nurse Vicky and House Changes

2001

"YOU ARE A *BULLY*," ANNE SCREAMS.

There it is again.

"I know, I know," I soothe her. "But you must listen to us this time, it's for your own good!"

District Nurse Vicky kneels in front of Anne's wheelchair. "Anne, please don't get upset. You know Chris is just doing his best, trying to look out for you and to care for you the best way he can. You need this catheter."

"He's ganging up on me. Everyone is, and it's all his doing! Chris, Dee – and now you? I will *not* have a catheter."

Anne's speech is so slurred and slow by this time, that it is extremely difficult to listen to her, stumbling through her words. Especially when she is so angry and upset.

"Just listen to me… I can't even speak properly anymore. Why are you taking away all my dignity?" Anne moans and closes her eyes.

Vicky sighs. "I tell you what, Anne. Why don't I arrange for you to go and visit the audio department at Frenchay Hospital, see what they say? We can get you a laptop computer so you can type a message on the screen, at your own pace. A computer-generated voice that can translate what you write. Would that be helpful?"

Anne nods.

"Great, I will set that up. In the meantime, let me organise for this catheter to be fitted. One less thing for Chris to think about."

Vicky smiles encouragingly at Anne, who nods again. She has no strength left to argue.

The computer gives Anne her voice back, but it takes a couple more weeks of near-daily visits from Dee, and efforts from both Vicky and myself, to get Anne to agree to the catheter.

"I can't feel the keys," the computer says in a monotone voice as Anne types.

"What?"

My heart sinks. The consultant said this might happen, but I am not expecting it to happen so soon.

Anne shakes her head, slowly, and stares at her keyboard, shoulders sloping forward, dejected. Even her computer can't communicate with us now.

"I thought I had more time," I say quietly to Dee that evening after she has said goodnight to Anne. Dee is with us most days at the moment. Helping us through the dark times. I don't want Anne to overhear us speaking, as I know she will be very upset to think that we are discussing her private issues.

It is the signals from her brain controlling her muscles that are getting weaker. If she is unable to type, she will be unable to communicate.

"I feel that this is the final phase, Dee." I choke back a sob.

"Perhaps the time has come to contact Simon," Deidre says.

Simon is the priest from Bath Abbey.

"I'm sure he wouldn't mind coming up and spending some time with you both, just so you have someone to talk to. It will probably do you both good."

As usual, this is one of Deidre's suggestions that proves beneficial.

Simon starts coming to us weekly. Besides Deidre, the carers and nurses, he is the only other person we see.

Twenty-Six

House Renovations

2001

As more and more equipment enters our world, I begin to feel a stranger in my own house. It has been such a nurturing, warm family space for so many years, but now it is rapidly being converted into a nursing home. When Anne had been walking and talking, it had been easy to pretend that life was just going to continue as before.

"I don't want social services around, Chris," Anne says one morning after a particularly restless night.

"They need to come to assess the house," I answer. "You know what the GP said. We need support services as I can't manage on my own. Getting you upstairs to bed is almost impossible now."

I think of the twenty minutes I spend every evening, sliding, half-supporting, half-pulling Anne up the stairs, step by step.

"Fine," Anne says. "Get them in. I won't do anything they say if I don't agree with it, though. I want to live a normal life in a normal house."

I look at her, sadly. Those days are long gone, but as always, Anne needs time to get used to the adjustments.

Anne's living quarters are duly moved downstairs. Two hoists are installed to lower and raise her into a wheelchair/disability chair. Sophisticated entry systems are installed.

Anne is resistant every step of the way. She doesn't want the changes, but finally accepts they need to happen. We have to look ahead in view of her worsening condition and need facilities built downstairs straight away. It takes a great deal of effort by myself, the doctor, district nurse and occupational therapist to persuade her this is the only way she can be properly looked after.

Leading from the kitchen door is the outside toilet attached to a substantial brick-built shed. We build an en-suite in place of the shed, and a utility area to replace the outside toilet, enabling Anne to be wheeled into the shower/loo. This is not a cheap option, and we had to dip into our ever-diminishing savings to fund the project, with costs in excess of £40,000.

In addition to our family home being pulled apart and rearranged, there are the daily and evening visits by the nurses. The house is a revolving door of doctors, carers, nurses, physios, occupational therapists and now Simon the priest.

I never have time to stop and think about how difficult it all is. I hadn't realised we would have to plan so far ahead all the time. The next challenge always seems to happen so rapidly there is no time to organise anything. I am on the move twenty-four seven, and my body begins to suffer the anxieties and pressures I experience daily. I feel even worse when I think what Anne must be going through. She has no control over anything and is paralysed, both physically and mentally, by all that is going on around her, invading her happiness and privacy.

"What fuss!" Anne says, while she can still communicate. "Do you know what they are suggesting now? A new car. The mobility car they originally made us buy, with the hoists, isn't good enough now, apparently."

I know that Anne is aggrieved at all the effort on her behalf.

"A swanky new VW Sedan with special hydraulic hoists means you can still get out and about outside, see the world, get some fresh air," says Dee, always the voice of reason.

"I still don't like it," Anne says. "Nothing is normal anymore – not even my car. And don't get me started on the expense…"

It is true. All these house amendments, new cars, specialist equipment, come at a cost, both emotionally and financially. In my eyes, though, every penny of it is well spent in order to make the last few years of Anne's life as comfortable as possible.

I am getting more and more tired with the daily demands of caring for someone with twenty-four-hour needs.

Night carers from Dorothy House (a hospice that later comes to mean so much to both of us) start coming in so that I can get some sleep and respite. Weekends, a time of relaxation and downtime for most families, came to be the worst time for me, as I was then left to cope on my own.

Twenty-Seven

Talking to Dee About Proposing to Anne

2002

Dee closes the door softly.

"She's asleep," she says. Dee sits down next to me, and I hand her the cup of tea I had made earlier.

"Tough day?" she asks as I close my eyes and tilt my head back against the armchair.

"One of the worst," I sigh.

"Stubborn, isn't she?" Dee chuckles, then hesitates. "Tell me about Anne. You know, about when you first met. What was she like when she was young? Only tell me if you feel happy to, of course."

I think about it. It has been a long time since I had thought about Anne as she was – young and vibrant. Not as she currently is.

"Well. It was love at first sight," I say, laughing, clutching my chest dramatically.

"Of course. All great love stories are." Dee laughs back. "How did you meet?"

"On a blind date, at a dance. The minute I set eyes on her, I knew my heart was taken. I had never met anyone like Anne. Intelligent, cultured and sophisticated… I knew it was going to be a hard fight to win her over. Her beauty was legendary."

"Still is!" Dee says, affectionately.

"Indeed," I agree.

Dee and I can see past the paralysis, the deterioration.

To us, Anne is still as beautiful as she has always been.

"Of course, I just knew she would be mine in the end. She was powerless in the face of my natural charm and wit," I say, with a cheeky twinkle in my eye.

"Big-head!"

"Convincing her parents of my charm was another thing entirely," I continue, ignoring her. "They were very Welsh, and very strict. They were very cautious about the company Anne kept. Every admirer was vetted. I remember when we were first courting, there was always a curfew in place, and her father Vernon would be waiting on the doorstep for her. Quite intimidating for someone like me! Also, just before we were married, Anne decided that she wanted to introduce me to her relatives in Llanrhystud and Aberystwyth. I felt like I was getting married into the Welsh mafia, and being given the once-over by the extended family! There were endless rounds of visits for afternoon tea. I was nervous the whole time. Anyway, I seemed to have passed the test."

"The whole thing sounds a bit daunting," Dee says.

"It was! Luckily I passed muster, and was accepted by the family."

"Thank goodness for that," Dee says.

"On top of the family scrutiny, I also had to fend off many of her admirers over the years. Including a French Count – some cad she met at the Sorbonne. She used to make me jealous with tales of her riding pillion on Count Xavier's motorbike, hurtling round Paris with her long blonde hair blowing in all directions." I chuckle. "Still can't believe she settled for me!"

"Well, I'm sure Anne's happy about that decision now. Do you think Count Xavier would be spoon-feeding her and mopping her brow with tenderness when she's had a distressing night?" Dee asks.

"True! No! He would be off, gallivanting in his fast cars. You are right, Anne was extremely lucky to have dodged the dodgy count!" I laugh, a little too loudly.

We hear a noise from Anne's bedroom, and both stop to listen. We are always on alert, in case we need to attend to Anne's needs. It's one of the more mentally exhausting aspects of looking after an incapacitated loved one.

There is silence, and we relax again.

"Fortunately, it all worked out OK, as it didn't take long to get to know her parents," I say. "Anne's dad was a real down-to-earth, no-frills-attached person, a highly skilled orthopaedic surgeon. I respected him for what he did for other people suffering from all kinds of injuries."

"I can see where Anne gets her caring side from, then. Where is he now?"

"Vernon died from cancer of the oesophagus on the first day of his retirement," I say, sadly. "He was only sixty."

"The very first day? What terrible luck!" Dee says, horrified.

"Yes, really, really tragic. We found ourselves in a difficult position at that time. I was married to Anne, working hard at my career. We had a new-born baby, and suddenly Anne found herself having to care for her mother, who had been looking forward to blissful retirement with Vernon. Anne and her mum were both quite devastated."

We sit there for a while in silence, thinking about the unfairness of life.

"Well, OK, that's the sad part. Where are the happy parts?" Dee says, always looking for the optimistic side of life.

"Well, I have lots of very happy memories driving from Devizes to Bath in my Morris van each week. Sometimes after a dance, I wouldn't reach my cottage in Potterne until the early hours of the morning! It was brilliant fun. And very tiring."

"That's true dedication. Or true love," Dee says, standing up to check in on Anne. She can't put that noise out of her mind.

Dee walks in to the kitchen and returns with a battered Quality Street tin full of home-made shortbread. She offers me one, which I gratefully accept. Dee's baking is second to none.

"True love indeed. I proposed to Anne on the night of 22nd November, 1963, at a dance aboard a naval training ship in Bristol Docks. It was a memorable night, in more ways than one," I say, biting into the buttery biscuit. It crumbles down my front. "Delicious," I remark, licking my fingers and pressing them onto the crumbs so I don't waste a morsel.

"Thank you," Dee says, smiling. "Your proposal sounds romantic. In what other way was it memorable?"

"Well, funny thing was, just after she'd said, '*Yes*,' there was another announcement. John F Kennedy had been assassinated riding in a motorcade in Dallas, Texas. It was a big deal! The celebrations ended immediately. I shall never forget that night and the repercussions. On the one hand, marvellous – in that Anne had agreed to be my wife – and on the other, terrible, resulting in the death of a great man."

"With you, Chris, there's always a story," Dee says, raising one eyebrow and smiling.

"That's true." I smile back. "Where would I be without my stories?"

"Well, keep them coming. I doubt Anne will be stirring any time soon. When I just checked, she was absolutely out for the count. Those stronger painkillers seem to be doing the trick," Dee says.

"Thank goodness," I reply. "She really needs some rest."

"How long after you met did you get married?" Dee asks, dunking her shortbread in her tea.

"Well, not that quickly. A couple of years. Anne is a very independent person, as you know," I say, meaningfully.

"Me and you both know!" Dee says.

"Yes, indeed. Here's a fun fact about Anne you might not be aware of. She has four A Levels!"

"Really?" Dee says.

"Yep. It was uncommon to be female and educated to such a level, in her time. Anne also has a degree from the Sorbonne. She can speak perfectly fluent French. She used to teach English to the French students in Bath until she entered the careers service and became a trainee youth employment officer in the careers office in Bristol. Wasn't that where you and her met?" I ask.

"Yes, it was! She just never talks about how you guys met. Or what a clever clogs she is! Funnily enough, she likes to keep personal things close to her chest," Dee says, wryly.

"Sounds just like her, indeed," I agree. "Well, it hasn't always been smooth sailing. I remember one particularly testing time for us. Anne was obtaining a qualification at a college in Sidcup just before we got married. She needed the qualification to allow her to follow her dream of looking after the disadvantaged and special needs children and young adults in our area, you see. So she was travelling back and forth to Sidcup from Bath, and I was working still in Devizes. Needless to say, our meetings were infrequent!"

"Gosh. That sounds like quite the ordeal. I imagine you had to work to keep the relationship fresh. Did you ever have doubts?" Dee asks.

"Often, Dee. But I'm glad I stuck with it. She is one of a kind," I reply.

"I'm glad you ended up with your lady," Dee says, placing her empty cup on the side table. "Enough reminiscing for tonight, I think. I'm heading home. See you tomorrow, Chris. If you need anything, you know where I am."

I watch her put her beige trench coat on.

"Thank you, Dee. For everything," I say gratefully.

I feel lighter, having travelled back down memory lane. I remember all the lovely things about Anne I fell in love with, back in the day.

It is an important thing to do at this difficult time, when life can feel relentless.

Twenty-Eight

Chris's Work

2002

"I was talking to Dee last night about how we met," I say chattily to Anne as I measure out her tablets the next morning.

Anne looks at me, and whispers, "Oh, yes?"

"Yes! It was lovely, actually, thinking back on it all. All those mad trips to the relatives in Wales. Life was so carefree then, back in 1965, wasn't it? Not a worry in the world, pootling about in that little British racing green Morris at fifty miles an hour."

"It was," Anne says, her mouth twisting into a semblance of a smile, accepting her medication.

"It was simpler then. You worked hard, you got married, you bought a house," I say wistfully. "Not like it is with youngsters these days."

I am thinking of Louisa. How is she ever going to be able to afford a house on her salary in this day and age? The house prices in Bath and surrounding areas are crazy.

I stroke Anne's hair and wipe her hands and arms with a wet cloth.

"We are a good partnership, you and me, darling. Do you remember how you pushed me to try and further my career?" I ask tenderly.

Anne nods.

"Not pushed. Encouraged…" she says, weakly, rolling her eyes at my use of language.

"Ha, yes. Encouraged. In your very persuasive 'Anne' way!" I agree, laughing. I still enjoy that we can have a laugh. Anne's dry wit never wavers.

Early in our marriage, Anne had always been concerned that I had been unable to further my education after I joined Sharps in 1958. I had been so hell-bent on returning to my beloved South Africa after my five-year management training course with Sharps, I had dismissed getting any further qualifications out of hand. When W H Bourlet sold to the Trebor Group, my settlement was more than sufficient to purchase a cottage in Bradford-on-Avon, roughly equidistant between Devizes and Bristol, where Anne worked. The unexpected merger between Bourlet's with Trebor put paid to those grand plans of travelling back to South Africa. Following the merger between Trebor and Sharps I was invited to be director of W H Bourlet, the confectionary and tobacco wholesaler in Devizes where I was working as a trainee with Sharps. My natural drive and ambition took over. Plans were shelved, my career took off, and South Africa had to take a backseat.

"You are the brains of this operation, really, aren't you my dear?" I say now, fondly, squeezing out the water into the bowl by her bed, and pulling her forward to wipe the back of her neck.

Anne nods, eyes scrunching in amusement.

"You could always see the bigger picture, right? It was you who pushed me to qualify as a Company Secretary in 1974 after I left Bourlet's and set up Doveton Press. Thank God you did. Otherwise we might not be enjoying all this luxury!"

I wave my hand around the bedroom, at our beautiful home stuffed to the rafters with all the equipment paid for by my canny investments and careful saving. If only I knew then that I was at risk of losing it all, after I lost her.

With Anne's support, I had started up a printing company in 1969 four years into our marriage. Doveton Press is now one of the largest printers in Bristol. I sold my stake when I joined Unilever and the computer industry in the eighties.

Not content with our own printing business, and with the prescience of foresight, Anne had also persuaded me to enrol onto a four-year degree equivalent course. It covered Administration, Law, Economics, Accountancy/Tax and Company Management. I progressed through the ranks of Associate of the Chartered Institute, later becoming a Fellow of the Institute. I was proud of my achievements, and more importantly, Anne was. Quietly steering from behind the scenes, I always like to think she made me the man I was always meant to be.

My new qualifications also meant I was able to make great inroads into the newly emerging computer industry. I worked at Apple Computers and then helped set up the Toshiba Computer Division. I was working at the Abbey as the first administrator and also running the Bath Cats and Dogs Home. I had to give all of this up when her condition worsened. My flourishing career ended abruptly at age sixty. I could tell she often had deep regrets about that, and I was careful to never complain about it when I was around her.

"Our life changed when our lovely Louisa came along," I say now. I lie her gently back against the pillows and throw the washcloth into the bowl of water. "There. Your night bath is all done."

"Do you remember when Louisa came? We were in chaos!" I say, not wanting to end our chat.

In 1977, now financially secure with both our careers doing well, we adopted Louisa six weeks after her birth in early October.

Anne smiles and closes her eyes.

"It was hard at first. You were still working in the careers service, and you were training to become a Relate counsellor. Goodness, we were busy! I remember looking after little Louisa when you were off doing your training courses in Rugby. How on earth did we cope?" I say in wonder.

"We just did. People just do," Anne says, slowly.

"I don't regret it for a second, do you?" I ask.

"Not one," she says.

I stroke her hair now, and say, "Do you remember our trip to South Africa, darling? That was quite a time, wasn't it?"

Anne nods, and says, "Tell me the story."

And I tell her the story again.

This was how we spend our days now. I reminisce about times past, and she listens, and nods. Sometimes she laughs. Often she cries.

Twenty-Nine

Anne's Last Holiday

2000

DURING ANNE'S LAST FEW YEARS, WE TRY TO KEEP things as normal as possible. Travel is something we both love to do, and we don't stop planning trips.

"I'm so sorry, darling," I say, as I enter the living room. Anne is watching a nature programme, one of the few things she enjoyed watching. She isn't very keen on all the modern programmes or soaps of the day, but she always has time for a David Attenborough documentary. She has several dogs dotted around her feet, and one on her lap. I stand at the door, watching her, a strong feeling of love washing over me.

"Sorry? What about?" Anne asks, not taking her eyes off the TV.

"I've had to cancel the Baltic cruise," I say, regretfully.

Anne presses the off button on the controller. The room is quiet.

I go and sit opposite to her on the sofa.

"But… our trip is in two days' time! We're all packed. The dogs are booked in. Why on earth did you cancel it?" Anne looks bewildered and disappointed.

"I made a discovery this morning about our schedule. The majority of the port stops are inaccessible. Our ship wouldn't be moored alongside the dock, but in the sound. This means we'd have to go ashore by tender. Which you know would be impossible, with you now permanently in the wheelchair."

"Oh," Anne says, quietly. She tuts. "You with your naval speak. Do you mean the ship couldn't come to shore, and I would have to be transported to dock by a smaller boat?"

"Yes, correct. Even if we did manage to get you to shore, then travelling by coach to places such as Stalingrad, Tallinn, St Petersburg, Helsinki… well, the coaches wouldn't be able to take you. We would have to find our own taxi, and this would be a pricey and unreliable option for consideration."

"OK. So what now?"

"We will still go away. I just need to research somewhere a little more suitable."

"I'm sorry, Chris," Anne says. "I'm such a nuisance. I know how much you were looking forward to this trip."

"Don't worry." I kiss the top of her head. "Any trip with you will be wonderful."

We decide to go to Tenerife. I do a lot of research and discover a special hospice there that caters for people with severe disabilities or recovering from serious injuries.

The swimming pool has hoists, and patients can receive treatment by specially trained physiotherapists. We travel with our own nurse from the practice, so that she can look after Anne twenty-four seven. A little break for me, too. This is not a cheap option but a necessary one. Just another cost of travelling with a person with a disability.

We have the most wonderful, relaxing holiday. My daughter Louisa and Andrew, her husband, have joined us. It's a great bonding time, and every day feels like a blessing.

This all changes on the return flight to Bristol from Tenerife. By now Anne has to be lifted into the fuselage of the aircraft on a special platform. On entering the cabin we find the front seats we have pre-booked (Anne needs the extra leg space) have been taken. After a few moments of confusion, it transpires we had been double-booked, and the current occupants won't budge. The only seats available are at the rear of the plane.

"How are we going to get her down there?" I say, crossly, pointing past the sea of passengers. The flight is packed.

"We normally have an adapted aircraft wheelchair on board to take her down the aisle, but, err... we don't seem to have one on this particular flight, I've just checked. I'm very sorry, sir," explains a red-faced cabin crew member.

After much discussion, Andrew, my six foot four son-in-law, ends up hoisting a distressed Anne over his shoulder, and performs a fireman's lift to reach the seats in the rear. Anne is placed in the cramped seats, and it becomes quickly obvious that this is not an ideal solution.

"I want to speak to the chief steward," I say, loudly. By this time, all the occupants of the plane are turning and staring. They want to know what the commotion is and worry about a delay.

The chief steward is summoned and the situation is taken in hand. He manages to persuade the occupants in the front seat that Anne would suffer greatly if she is left cooped up at the back of the plane for four hours.

Back Anne goes, up on Andrew's shoulder, as he repeats the exercise and manoeuvres her back down to the front of the plane. Anne, by this point, is in real pain and discomfort after a very happy holiday, which she had thoroughly enjoyed with all her family. We fly back in near-silence. We are disappointed it had to end like this.

Sadly, this was to be her last trip away.

Thirty

God

2002

"WE NEED TO TALK ABOUT GOD," I SAY, LOOKING AT her imploringly.

Anne turns her head away from me.

"No," she mumbles, closing her eyes. This is usually the cue that the discussion is closed.

"But it's important, Anne, to know how you feel."

"Well, what do *you* feel about God, Chris? Huh? Is this fair? Do you feel like he is looking out for you? I'm not sure he's looking out for me," Anne says, flatly.

I sit in silence. This is not the direction I want this conversation to go.

"We don't know God's plan, Anne. The only thing I have to cling on to at the moment is my faith. Don't take that away from me."

The subject of religion is a touchy one in our household. I have always held a strong faith. It has guided me and been a strong part of my life for as long as I can remember. Anne is, unsurprisingly, much more private in her thoughts about God. Yes, she comes with me to Bath Abbey, and supports my singing and my interest. Still, she remains quiet on the subject.

I know that she has mixed feelings.

The priest, Simon, comes weekly to visit us. Anne always refuses to talk with him about religion. I suspect if she has any faith at all, she does not have much faith in her faith, at this time. I myself come very close to wavering. I spend a lot of time thinking about what God means to me, and the Church. I am particularly confused about religion in relation to death. I want to talk about this all the time, get some clarity on it. Anne doesn't, however, and this is difficult for us.

I am not sure I can forgive God, for what he has done, putting us in this situation.

Simon and I spend many hours discussing my concerns during his weekly visitations. I realise all I want to do is talk. In this, I am the opposite of Anne, who keeps her inner feelings to herself.

I never stop praying, not once. I pray to God to give me strength to manage Anne's strength of character. She has started putting her foot down about the slightest thing. Any recommendation the doctor or nurse puts forward in terms of her treatment she fights, tooth and nail. A decision that should have been agreed in an afternoon stretches out over three, four weeks as we argue about what course of action would be best for her. She never explains how she feels about this, she just says a blanket, "No!"

It is up to me (and Dee) to convince her and bring her around.

Deidre and I become masters of deception, trying to think of different ways of presenting the particular treatment plan she is objecting to in the best light.

One day, we find ourselves back to the catheter debate:

"You need a catheter and a bag, Anne."

"No, absolutely not! I refuse to be fitted with one of those things. You can't expect me to lose my dignity," she says, that look of determination fixed on her face.

"But, Anne, please think about the alternative. Is there any dignity in that?"

"I won't think about it."

And on and on this would go, for days, weeks…

"See, I told you it was a terrible idea," Anne says, as I struggle daily with the maintenance of the bag. She has finally given in.

"But, can't you see there is no other option?" I reply, mildly.

Then comes the final straw.

Thirty-One

The PEG

December 2002

"A PEG? What does that mean?"

We are talking with Dr Bateman, the neurologist.

"Your disease is at a stage where you can only swallow liquids, now. Without a PEG, you will starve to death."

"How can a PEG help?" I ask.

"A PEG is an endoscopic procedure where a tube is passed into a patient's stomach through the abdominal wall. This tube will bypass Anne's oesophagus, and she won't have to swallow anymore."

"That sounds like major surgery," I say, panicked. "Anne is very weak. She'd never get through the anaesthetic."

Anne makes a noise and I look at her. She raises her hand and points at me, eyes imploring. I know what this look means. It's her way of saying she wants the conversation to stop. The discussion about her current condition ends right now.

There is silence in the room, but my mind is whirring. What if the procedure goes wrong?

"That is all I can tell you at the moment," Dr Bateman says. "It's an easy procedure, done under a mild sedation, if that puts your mind at ease. Less than a three per cent chance of anything going wrong. But I understand if you need a little time to think about it."

Anne looks at the doctor and moves her mouth in an attempt to speak. The doctor puts her ear close to Anne's mouth.

"Will this PEG prolong my life?" Anne whispers.

She takes Anne's gnarled, twisted hand.

"There is no guarantee, Anne, like with all these things. It will most probably prolong your life, yes. You will be more comfortable, and the likelihood of pneumonia will be diminished. It's your choice. As your doctor, I recommend it as your best option right now."

"I'll think about it," Anne says, with a twisted half-smile.

I glance at her sharply. I know what that kind of smile means. I shiver at the memory of the catheter fight. Anne will never agree to the PEG. She is ready to sign her own death warrant.

Inside, my heart breaks into a million pieces. We have come to the end of the road.

Thirty-Two

Dorothy House and Princess Anne

2002/Present Day

I AM OFTEN ASKED WHETHER THERE WERE ANY moments of joy during this difficult time.

The respite visits to the Dorothy House Hospice near Bath were where I sought solace and, I suppose, a strange kind of joy. Here, Anne is pampered to within an inch of her life. She is hoisted into a special bath, enjoys massages. It is a safe space for her to vent her frustrations, feel love and compassion, and to not have to rely on me. Everyone there is suffering from cancer, brain tumours, strokes, motor neurone disease; all similar symptoms to Ataxia.

Here, Anne is no longer the only patient.

Towards the end, when Anne stays more and more frequently as her needs increase, I find that I can't stay away. For up to four days a week, Anne is able to get away from her normal life, have a day out in the day care centre, doing completely normal things surrounded by people who really understand what she is going through. It is like a complete holiday from the horror of her everyday existence.

"She can be completely honest here," I explain to Dee on one of our numerous walks around the beautiful grounds. "Anne doesn't have to contend with me or anyone telling her what to do all the time. She doesn't have to keep her spirits up here if she doesn't want to," I continue.

"When she goes…"

Deidre and I both swallow, blinking back our tears, the thought unbearable.

"I doubt I will be able to keep away, it's a tonic for me too," I finish.

"It must be wonderful having a doctor on call twenty-four seven," Deidre says, encouragingly. "It takes the pressure off you."

"Yes, and she gets rewarded here. Not constantly being reminded of her battles with her health, but with extra comfort and succour and love… extra love," I say, with gratitude. "Did I tell you, Deidre, what happened last week? It was extraordinary. You know Princess Anne is the patron of Dorothy House Hospice? Well, she popped in on one of her annual visits, and luckily Anne happened to be in that day. Would you believe that Princess Anne stopped to talk to her? It absolutely made my Anne's day, she was overjoyed! She even talked to me," I say, proudly.

"What did she say?" Deidre is almost as excited as I am.

"Well," I laugh, "Princess Anne asked me what I do as a job. I explained that I manage the Dogs and Cats home in Bath, and do you know what she said?"

"Tell me!"

"'Oh! So, you are responsible for all my birds being killed by these feral cats!' So I answer back, 'Well, actually we do have a feral cat colony in the Dogs and Cats home, and we rescue all these feral dogs and cats roaming around. Then they get retrained and rehomed if they aren't too bad. So, it's an improvement if you think about it,'" I say.

Dee gasps and says, "You didn't! What did she say to that?"

"Well, this is the extraordinary bit – then Princess Anne shook my hand and said, 'Oh, that *does* sound like a good thing. I wish we had one up near where we are!'"

Dee and I both laugh.

"What an extraordinary conversation to have with a real-life princess!" Dee says.

"And a little moment of delight for my own princess," I add.

And so, we continue our walk in silence, happy that our humble Anne, who gave so much of her life to looking after and loving the animals at the Dogs and Cats Home, had been lucky enough to witness that conversation with Princess Anne.

I think fondly back to my days spent in the day care unit at the hospice. I came to know many of the partners, and I was able to understand the sacrifices they were having to make in order to give their loved one's end-of-life support and love. I feel humbled that patients trusted me with their innermost feelings of despair, knowing that they would soon die. They would open up about their lives, their hopes and fears. It was a privilege to discuss 'End of Life' with them and share my own experience. There was a wonderful bond and trust between us.

At the end of each day, I would have a 'post-mortem' with the hospice team, and revisit the time we had spent with patients to see if there was any way we could improve the quality of care for them, or indeed their carers. Sometimes we would share our faith and pray together.

At times, Tuesday could be a sad day, when someone didn't turn up. We all knew the reason for their absence. This was particularly hard when I had personally formed a strong bond with a patient.

My time at Dorothy House was very rewarding in so many ways and taught me a great deal about putting something back into life in helping others.

Thirty-Three

Grief

Present Day

I HAVEN'T EVEN GOT TO ANNE'S DEATH YET, BUT MY grief at her dying started the day Anne was diagnosed.

We knew she wasn't going to get better, and that was a tough thing to live with. It could be said that when it eventually happened and she died, I was freed from the bounds of managing her life, and then her death. Nothing could be further from the truth.

I thought I was free, but I had entered another sort of prison, one that affected my mind and my sanity. I had been abandoned again. Firstly by my mother. Then my mother replacement: my wife Anne. A bitter pill to swallow.

I have terrible problems with saying goodbye, even now.

I feel vulnerable all the time, and that is a difficult thing for me to say. Yet, here I am talking about things that

I have never shared with anyone, never felt comfortable talking about. My stiff upper lip is wavering. Now it feels like the right time to do so, as it's part of my story. My story about dealing with love and loss and how to find the light again. My personal journey of grief.

When Anne died, I entered a period of my life I call the wilderness. I am sorry to say that I did not behave in an admirable and honourable way.

It is the most regrettable period of my life...

Thirty-Four

Anne's Death

14th December 2002

I AM A BELIEVER.

I can say that, now, with conviction.

In Christ, what happens, and in the strength he has given me in so many ways.

My journey with Christ and my belief has been a complicated one.

I look down at Anne. She is dying. She has been dying for ten years. I guess we all have, in a way.

The nurses are packing up their equipment, tucking Anne in a final time and preparing to leave for the day.

"Goodnight, Chris. Please call us if you need anything. Especially if you're frightened or have any worries."

"I'm scared now," I say.

I haven't said this out loud to anyone before.

"I'm worried about her breathing. It doesn't seem right." I look at Anne, her face pale and pinched in the twilight.

"I know. I share your concerns. We've made her as comfortable as possible." The nurse approaches me, leans in closer and lowers her voice. "I don't think it will be much longer." She gives me a squeeze on the arm as she turns to leave with her colleague.

The nurses are gone, and I am alone. Thank goodness for Penny, Anne's beloved canine companion, asleep next to her in her usual spot.

I can also sense the end of Anne's mortal time on earth is approaching. The fear clutches at my heart. I'm not strong enough to do this. She can't leave me. She can't leave me on my own.

I kiss Anne gently, and pull the door to as I back out of her room. I need a little time to go upstairs to pray. I don't know what else to do.

"Please, Lord, relieve Anne of her suffering," I whisper, hands clenched in panic and desperation. "Please embrace her. Take her into your hands. I know in my heart you have prepared a banquet for her, a seat at your table. May she rest in peace forever. Amen."

I know what I am asking. My understanding is with God. Only he can release her from her suffering, but the end of her suffering will be the start of mine. Selfishly, I can't bear to think of life without her.

An overwhelming urge to be by her side comes over me.

I enter her room and my eyes are instantly drawn to an image of Christ above her bed. The air feels different. I walk to her side and look down. I place the back of my hand against her cool cheek.

Under the watchful eye of a God she didn't ever talk about, she has left me to join him.

My Anne is gone. She is sixty years old.

Thirty-Five

Thoughts on Anne's Death

14th December 2002

I SIT THERE IN SILENCE, BESIDE ANNE'S BED. I BEND my head in prayer. I feel strangely calm after the initial panic of realising she has slipped away.

Anne had been insistent that I was prepared for this moment. She has donated her brain to research. She wanted to help other sufferers of neurological diseases, such as Ataxia, Motor Neurone, Alzheimer's, and this was the best way she knew how. Giving, even in death.

Numb, on autopilot, I call the Royal United Hospital. Her brain needs to be removed within an hour of her death in order to be transported to Queen Square Hospital in London, the National Hospital for Neurology and Neurosurgery. The ambulance is on its way.

I have a few minutes to sit with my beloved wife whilst I wait.

"Come here, Penny," I whisper.

I cradle Anne's dog.

There is a flurry of activity as the doctor arrives and pronounces Anne dead. He issues a death certificate and I leave the room as he prepares her body for conveyance to the hospital.

Everyone leaves. Anne has been taken.

I sit by her empty bed and think.

Anne's body and soul had been broken. In all ways. As a Relate counsellor, Anne had often mentioned this feeling of being broken by the sadness around her and her efforts to help. In later life, she had been broken herself with her disease. Her body had been broken for all of us, in a way. Like bread, to symbolise the body of Christ.

I know that I will go through the same breaking process in the months and years to come. I try and take comfort in the obvious parallel. Christ also broke for us. But my faith is being tested to the extreme. Why did my lovely Anne have to break? My Princess Grace?

It is only later that I come to realise. To understand who you are, you have to be shattered to rebuild. You have to go through the process of looking back in order to move forward.

But for now I can't see beyond my grief.

The start of my deep depression has begun.

Thirty-Six

Immediately After Anne's Death

9.30pm 14th December 2002

I CALL LOUISA. I DON'T KNOW WHAT ELSE TO DO.

"Oh, OK, thanks for letting me know."

Louisa sounds neutral at best.

Her response takes me a bit by surprise.

The next words, even more so.

"She's won," Louisa says.

"Sorry?" I ask in bewilderment. These are not the words I am expecting to hear from my daughter when I tell her the news of her mother's death.

"Mum. She's won. The last thing she said to me before I left for Meribel to work at the chalet. She said, 'You *will* be back for Christmas, won't you, Louisa?'"

Louisa laughs dryly.

"Oh," I say, quietly.

I glance automatically at the calendar on the wall. The date is 14th December.

Louisa will indeed be back for Christmas.

"I told her straight, you know," Louisa continues. She is gabbling a bit now. Her speech is fast and breathless.

"'Mum, that won't be possible,' I said. 'The chalet is fully booked and we can't leave...'" Louisa sighs and her breathing slows down. "Of course, that wasn't good enough for her."

Louisa laughs again, hollowly.

"Mum doesn't let things drop. Mum always wins."

I can hear her ragged breathing on the end of the line. I imagine her plucking at the strand of blonde hair that always falls in front of her forehead, stretching it out in front of her face.

"Yes, she does, Louisa," I say.

I correct myself. "She did."

We sit there, two people in different countries, connected by our voices over a line. I have never felt more alone.

"You know, it's funny," Louisa says. Her voice catches. I can hear the swallow of tears in her throat.

"I had a conversation with Andrew about it. I made him promise me that he would come back to England with me if she died. I just didn't believe she would. One part of my brain knew she was very ill, of course," she says, openly sobbing now. "The other part told me that would be the last time I would ever see her again."

"Oh, Louisa."

I don't know how to comfort her.

"I didn't realise that she would win the bet this time. The only important time."

"Oh, darling," I say helplessly.

I am at a loss for words. It is hard enough having to deal with Anne's passing without hearing the grief and regret in my beloved daughter's voice.

"You know, just before I left the house to catch the train to Meribel, I tried to say goodbye to Mum properly. I went to her room, and I tried to say my goodbyes."

Louisa's tone is more brusque now. I can hear from the change in her voice that she's now standing. I imagine her pacing the corridor in the chalet, pulling at that strand of hair.

"I couldn't. I didn't get a chance to say it. Nurse Vicky came in with her meal."

Louisa has pulled herself together.

"I never got to say a proper goodbye," she says quietly, again.

She sounds emotionless now. I don't know what's more worrying.

"Oh, Louisa, of course you did. You said a proper goodbye, I know you did. Mum knew. That's why she made her bet. She had made peace with the fact her time was coming."

My words, although true, sound hollow. I am trying to make her feel better, when there is nothing I can say.

There is nothing anyone can say. Our world has been torn apart.

Thirty-Seven

Louisa
Hearing About Her
Mum's Death

9.30pm 14th December 2002

"I'M SO SORRY, LOUISA. SHE'S GONE."

I sit in silence, hearing the words my dad is saying, but not really registering them.

"Gone where?" I ask.

There is a huge pause.

"Heaven, my darling. She passed away peacefully at 9pm tonight."

"Oh, OK. Thanks for letting me know," I say this automatically, almost politely.

I can tell Dad is surprised at my emotionless response.

We chat briefly about this and that, my mind in total shock at the news. I didn't get to say a proper goodbye. I am angry, devastated, numb. I don't know what to do with all my emotions.

Of course I should have expected this day to come, but I somehow never thought it would. I had no idea about Mum's illness until the summer of 1994. I was seventeen at the time and taking my A Levels. I remember Dad's words clearly, what he had said at the time.

"Mum's just having an MRI scan to clear something up. Nothing to worry about, we are just waiting for the results."

And I didn't worry. He had told me there was nothing to worry about, so I went about my life, preoccupied with the usual teenage triangle of boys, friendships, studying.

One day I noticed Mum was finding it difficult to walk and keep her balance. A trolley appeared suddenly out of nowhere to help her move around downstairs. Her bed was moved to the ground floor. Medical equipment arrived almost daily.

It would seem that there was something to worry about after all.

A random thought now pops into my head, my mind wandering whilst Dad talks about funeral arrangements and flowers.

I think about the last time I saw Mum drive.

Mum has a lovely red BMW. The absolute pride of her life.

"Louisa, darling. Are you busy this afternoon?"

I suppress the urge to tell her that I am always busy.

I sigh. We haven't spent much time together recently

with everything going on, so I put down my pen and look up at her.

"No, Mum, not very," I say, trying to sound enthusiastic. "What do you fancy doing?"

"Well…" Mum seems hesitant. This is most out of character for her. She is normally a very decisive person.

"Do you fancy taking a trip to Alexandra Park in my car and testing my driving? It's been a while since I have felt confident enough to drive alone – I just need someone to tell me how I'm doing."

"Of course." I smile up at her. "Let's go."

I grab her keys and off we set in her smart red BMW. I love driving this car and feel happy as we make our way to Alexandra Park. When we get there, we change seats and set off. Mum grips the wheel tightly.

"How am I doing?" she asks, halfway round the park.

I realise she has noticed me hanging tightly on to my seatbelt, as we narrowly miss shooting off down the steep bank again.

"I think we had better stop now, Mum," I suggest gently with a smile.

Mum stops the car, puts on the handbrake and looks at me. Suddenly we both burst out laughing, tears rolling down our cheeks.

We change seats again, and I drive back home.

I am not as happy on the drive back that day. I know that Mum will never drive again.

Another thing that she cannot do.

Of course she still works, even though she cannot drive. I start taking her to the college at Radstock, where she is a tutor. I help her from the car park to the classroom where she is met by her friend Caroline. Everyone pretends everything is normal, even though it is not.

And now nothing will ever be normal again. No more memories will be made. The loss is too great and I am overwhelmed. Dad is still talking to me on the phone. He is being very detailed and I can't take it all in.

"Dad. I'm sorry. I can't think about any of that now. I'll… I'll call you later."

I put the phone down to Dad. I sit there quietly. I pick the phone up again.

"Ed?" I can't keep the tears from dripping off the end of my nose, and I sniff.

"What is it, Louisa?"

Ed is a family friend. He knows Mum, and also happens to be a Samaritan. I don't know what to do apart from call him. I am numb with shock and I have no idea what I should do next. Maybe he can help me.

"Mum has gone, Ed. Passed away. Died. Tonight. Just now. Help me. Tell me. What do I do? I don't know what to do."

There is a shocked brief pause. I think of him standing there, on the other end of the line, with his kind eyes and cheerful face. It brings me some comfort whilst I wait for his answer.

"Louisa, you know what to do," Ed says. "You have to go home."

"But I have only been here in Meribel for two weeks! I can't let the family down. I have so much work to do…" I am gabbling.

"Louisa, no. You have to go home. This family will cope without you at the chalet. Your family might not." He paused to let the message sink in. "I'm so sorry," he continued, more softly. "She was a wonderful woman. Go home and celebrate that fact with your loved ones."

I put the phone down. Ed is absolutely right.

I have to go home.

Thirty-Eight

Louisa and Anne
Last Time We See Each Other

1st December 2002

"I'm really excited, Mum! The ski chalet is so luxurious, much nicer than any chalet I have worked at before," I chatter as I bustle around Mum, making her comfortable, popping her straw into her glass of water and holding it up to her dry lips.

Mum can barely suck the water up the straw. I notice but don't say anything, wiping down the support equipment surrounding her bed and tucking her duvet more tightly around her.

"Back for Christmas, Louisa?" she types out slowly on her computer.

I sigh. I sit on the edge of the bed and hold her hand.

"Mum. We've spoken about this. You know that won't be possible this year. The chalet is fully booked, Andrew and I need the money, and we can't leave. We have committed to the job."

She looks at me, blinking heavily. She presses return. The question repeats. I look back at her. I kiss her on the forehead and leave her to rest.

Later I speak to Andrew.

"There was something odd about the way she was so insistent, Andrew."

"What about, you going back to Bath for Christmas? She knows that's impossible, doesn't she?" Andrew says.

"But… what if she dies?" My heart lurches as I say this.

"She won't," Andrew answers.

"If she does die," I gulp, "you will come back with me, won't you?"

I am panicky all of a sudden, the idea of Mum dying and Andrew not being by my side looming large in my mind.

"Of course, you silly sausage. But I won't have to, because she won't die." Andrew kisses me on my nose.

Like me, he also believes she will live forever. She has so far.

In my heart, though, I know.

This is the last time I will ever see her alive again.

When I arrived in the UK for the funeral, Vicky the district nurse takes me to one side.

"I'm so sorry, Louisa, for your loss. She really was a wonderful woman. It has been a privilege to take care of her these past few months."

I squeeze her hand gratefully and open my mouth to thank her.

"She did say something odd to me, though," Vicky continues.

"She told me that she would never see you again," Vicky says, with an awkward laugh.

"She said, 'If I can get on with it before Christmas, dying that is, then at least I know I've won.'"

Vicky looks at me.

"I never asked her what she meant by that. Do you know?"

I shake my head mutely. I am numb and mortified.

Thirty-Nine

Louisa
A Christmas Delivery

1st December 2002

"SUE, I HAVE A HUGE FAVOUR TO ASK YOU." I AM cramming a sandwich into my mouth as I scribble down more chores onto my ever-expanding list of things to do before I leave for Meribel to work at the chalet.

"Anything, Louisa. What is it?" Sue's voice is as warm as always over the phone. I like Sue enormously. I used to work for her as a nanny some years previously and she has always been so kind to me.

"I am away for the next few months, and so I was wondering if you would be kind enough to organise a Christmas sack to be delivered on Christmas Day to Mum and Dad?"

"No problem at all!"

Phew. One more thing ticked off my huge to-do list.

Or so I thought.

Forty

Louisa
A Christmas Return

20th December 2002

"I WOULD LIKE TO RETURN THESE AUDIOBOOKS please." My voice is hoarse and low, and I don't want to look at the kindly lady doing returns in Waterstones.

"Is there anything wrong with them? What's the reason for the return?" the nice lady asks, turning the carefully chosen gifts over in her hands, checking them.

"No. No. Nothing wrong with them. Sorry…"

I have started to cry and she looks up in concern.

"What's the matter, dear?"

She is so kind, I can't hold back.

"They… those were for my mum. For Christmas."

"But Christmas hasn't even come round yet. Why don't you give them to her?"

"She died. She died last week and she never got to listen to them."

I don't know why I am telling the lady all this, but something about her makes me feel safe.

The lady puts the audiobooks down and grasps my hands. She looks at me intently.

"I am so, so sorry, dear. I'm sorry for asking. We have never had someone return an unopened item because the recipient has passed away. I wasn't expecting that to be your reason."

I dash away my tears.

"I always like to be unique," I say, smiling.

She smiles back and continues the refund transaction in respectful silence.

When I get home I remember that I also have to cancel the flower delivery I had arranged to arrive monthly whilst I was away. The first order had never reached her.

Another difficult conversation.

I cry and cry that night. So many things Mum didn't get to see or open or experience and now never will.

Forty-One

Louisa
Clearing the House After
Mum's Death

December 2002

IT TAKES A SINGLE WEEK TO CLEAR ALL OF MUM'S belongings and remove them from the house. One week.

I watch as hoists are dismantled, the sophisticated door entry system is taken out, the waterbed is collected. I grab black bin liners and start throwing away all the smaller medical paraphernalia.

I look at Dad. He is clutching the Mangar.

"I used to hate this thing," he says, sadly. "It signified a time when she started to fall. When I couldn't get her up on my own. At the end, I missed it. I missed having to use it. It meant she wasn't moving around on her own anymore."

I walk over to him, gently take the dreaded Mangar out of his hands and place it on the pile of equipment in a box ready to be removed. I give him a hug.

"Are we doing this too soon?" I whisper.

"Why, do you feel like it is?" Dad asks in surprise.

"It feels like we are trying to erase all memory of her. A bit," I say.

Dad looks at me. "But… I don't want to remember her like this. Reduced to a bunch of medical equipment and house alterations. I want the house to return to something I recognise. Happier times, with happier memories."

He is right, of course.

I continue packing with renewed vigour. Mum would have hated it if we had kept her beloved house looking like a hospital. She would have also wanted our memories of her to be of her spirit and her kindness and determination.

"The sitting room feels like a morgue," I say sadly.

Dad agrees. We look at it.

"Let's get it back to looking like a home," he says.

Forty-Two

The Funeral

End of December 2002

THE FUNERAL IS SIMPLE, HELD AT HAYCOMBE Cemetery Church. I had always imagined Anne's funeral at Bath Abbey; but we hadn't worshipped there for a while, and even Louisa said it didn't feel right.

We use the priest from Dorothy House, as well as the rector from the Abbey. Anne had a great affinity with them both. After the service, she is taken to the crematorium which is below the church overlooking the beautiful countryside. It's a very simple funeral. Anne wouldn't have wanted anything else.

So saying, more than a hundred and fifty people attend. It brings tears to my eyes, seeing how loved Anne was, even to the end.

It is all done. The last vestige of medical equipment has left the house. Louisa has brought flowers over, her favourite, and a cake. Louisa and I sit quietly in the empty-feeling sitting room, having a cup of tea.

"I can still feel her here," I say.

"Me too," Louisa replies.

"You are staying for a while, yes?" I ask, hopefully.

Louisa puts her cup of tea down carefully.

"Andrew and I – we are returning to France."

"What, so soon?" I spill a bit of my tea as I place my cup back on the saucer. Louisa automatically hands me a linen napkin. She can't really look at me.

"I'm sorry," Louisa says, quietly. "But there is nothing more I can do here. And Andrew and I need to go back and work."

I don't say anything for what feels a long time.

"What will I do?" I finally ask.

"Well, you have your gym," Louisa says, encouragingly. "You have Simon from the Abbey. Maybe you could take up singing again?"

I look at Louisa, still clutching the tea-filled saucer in one hand and the napkin in the other.

"And you could always come out and visit us! Yes, that would be a jolly thing to do. Come and visit us in February or March before we come back. The trip would do you good."

"Yes," I say. "Yes, maybe it would."

Forty-Three

Louisa and Meribel

March 2003

ANDREW AND I RETURN TO MERIBEL AND STAY UNTIL the end of March.

We throw ourselves into working hard and enjoying as much of the remaining ski season as we can. I try not to think about Mum, and I especially try not to think about Dad, all alone in that house without her.

We speak often.

"I have booked my ticket," Dad tells me one day.

"Where?" I ask in surprise.

"To France!" he exclaims. "I'm coming to see you, remember?"

I had forgotten I had asked him to join us. I am happy about the idea of seeing him, I have missed him so much. But I know that seeing him will trigger emotions in me that I have so far managed to keep suppressed. I want him to come, but I dread it at the same time.

"I look forward to it." I keep my voice cheerful and we make arrangements. He is coming for ten days.

Later that day I travel up the mountain in the gondola. It is the peak of the season and the cabin is packed with people. I look at the green tips of the trees, poking out of the unblemished snow as we travel quietly up the mountain. I burst into uncontrollable sobs. I can't breathe. My legs feel shaky like I have run a marathon, my stomach twists in knots.

"Louisa, are you OK?" my friend Tina from Australia asks me in concern, grabbing my arm. I turn to her and cry into her neck, tears running down her ski jacket.

"I miss my mum," I say, not caring who can hear.

I feel safe saying this to Tina. I know she understands. Her own mum died two weeks ago.

"Me too," she says quietly, and we cling to each other, not caring about the stares and concerned glances of the other passengers.

We continue up the mountain, the air muffled and quiet apart from our sniffs and gulps of grief.

Dad arrives in France, and I am more happy than sad. He is outwardly cheerful and appears to be coping. The relief I feel is immense.

"I'm going shopping, after I've been skiing," he says, every morning.

"Wonderful. Have fun. Take your credit card! The prices are not to be believed in town," I say, laughing and rolling my eyes.

The first day he arrives home laden with bags, I am thankful that he is able to find joy in simple things like shopping for new clothes.

The second and third day, I am still happy but getting slightly concerned.

By the end of the ten-day visit, I am gripped by a terrible anxiety that threatens to overtake my feelings of grief.

I look at the new suitcase he has just brought home.

"Why do you need another suitcase, Dad?" I ask, tentatively.

"Well," he laughs, slightly guiltily, "I need to get all these home."

We stand and silently survey the spoils of his recent shopping spree. Beautiful French silk and leather skin tailored shirts, high shine shoes, a goatskin jacket. All laid out on the bed in a tantalising tableau.

"Gorgeous. When and where are you going to wear them?" I ask.

Dad is silent.

"I don't know," he answers, honestly.

He never does wear them. He takes them home in his extra suitcase and hangs them in his wardrobe where Mum's clothes used to be, where they hang, unworn, until he moves.

I try and fill the empty hole that Mum has left in another way. I start to eat. And enter the most miserable period of my life.

Forty-Four

Louisa and Weight Gain

2003

MY GRIEF STRETCHES OUT BEFORE ME. I DON'T KNOW what to do with myself. When my work finishes in Meribel I return to the UK.

I am a clothing size twelve when I arrive.

My appetite starts to increase. I try and eat away my sorrow. It's the only explanation.

I am overwhelmed with the choice of childhood treats that were not available to me in France. Scones, toast and butter, Battenberg cake, salty crisps, bars upon bars of Dairy Milk chocolate. All delicious, comforting and irresistible.

I eat and eat, trying to push out the sadness with soothing carbs. I jump several clothing sizes rapidly: twelve, fourteen, sixteen. I learn these sizes all mean different things depending on the brand. I try and squeeze myself into unforgiving jeans, I tug and pull at them and burst into tears at the sight of myself in the dressing room.

I soon realise a size sixteen limits my choices of clothing. Nothing fits. I don't know who I am, or how to dress.

"Darling," my dad says to me one day as I am sitting on my bedroom floor, weeping at not being able to pull on a pair of shorts. "I think it's time you went to see Dr Muddiman. Don't you?"

"Why?" I turn on him angrily. "For diet pills?"

"No, of course not! You are beautiful, whatever the number on the clothing labels. No, I mean I don't think you are very happy, are you?"

"Of course I'm not happy. My mother's dead," I wail.

"I'll make you an appointment." Dad closes the door and I hear him downstairs talking to the doctor's surgery.

I am prescribed antidepressants for the first time in my life. I cry again in the doctor's surgery.

Dr Muddiman was the doctor who looked after Mum in the last days of her life. Even that connection to her is unbearable to me.

Forty-Five

Louisa
South Africa

January 2004

A YEAR PASSES IN A BLUR.

Dad makes a plan.

We are to go to South Africa.

"Something to cheer us up, darling. I think a change of scenery would do us all the world of good," he says, encouragingly. "I have always wanted to show you where I grew up. South Africa is such an important part of my life, and I think you might enjoy meeting all the relatives. Get a sense of your history and your heritage!" Dad squeezes my shoulder.

I still feel numb, but I agree. It feels too exhausting not to.

"Don't worry, darling, you won't have to do anything, I will see to it all."

Dad arranges this marvellous trip. We travel to the Kruger National Park Game Reserve. The itinerary is full, and we go everywhere and we meet everyone. Throughout the beginning of the trip I don't know where to put myself. I feel uncomfortable and out of sorts, and my heart isn't in it. Dad tries his best to keep me jolly and upbeat, but I can't even pretend to be happy. The stay in Cape Town particularly is not a great success. We are both still in deep shock over Mum's death.

Dad racks his brains.

"How can we pull ourselves out of these doldrums?" he asks. "I know! I have a brilliant idea. Let's go and see Cousin Gilly in Plettenberg Bay. You will love her," he says.

I smile wanly. I'm not sure I love anything anymore.

It turns out Dad is right.

Cousin Gilly is the turning point in my grieving journey. She is warm and wonderful and understands how Dad and I are suffering. She sees me massaging my neck one day.

"Are you in pain, Louisa?" she asks. "It's quite common for grief to manifest itself in aches and pains in the body. I have a wonderful chiropractor. Let me book you in."

I go to the chiropractor nearly every day during my time with Gilly. The excruciating pains in my neck and shoulder gradually ease, as well as my overwhelming sadness.

Gilly and I spend hours together in the surf. I find this so soothing for my mind, body and soul. The sea washes away my tears and some of my sadness. I start to find joy in the simple things again.

Dad and I return to England re-energised and ready to start the next chapter of our lives without Mum.

It gets easier but it never goes away. My bouts of severe depression continue for over two years. I will never get over Mum's death and the way she died. It takes me seven years to feel able to talk about her again in any sort of meaningful way. She was such a wonderful person – it is too painful to even try. On my better days, I feel blessed to have experienced so much love for her that the pain is so raw. At other times I am angry that she was taken away from me.

So many ebbs and flows of emotion, like the surf I took such comfort in.

Forty-Six

Chris After Anne's Death

2003

I ENTER A BLEAK PERIOD OF MY LIFE.

It's all a bit of a blur. I only know what Louisa tells me, what my credit card statements reveal, the deep regret and shame that I carry with me now.

After the funeral, clearing the house, the hustle and bustle that goes hand in hand with organising someone's life after death, there is nothing. No friends, no faith, no hope. There isn't even Louisa, as she leaves Bath and returns to France shortly after Anne dies.

I lose contact with the outside world. That loss of contact had started, really, when Anne was ill. The only people we encountered then were the wonderful support staff who came daily to the house to help care for Anne.

I am heartened when I reconnect with friends and family after Anne's death in the immediate aftermath, but they soon dwindle to nothing again as they move on with their own lives. We never have visits from the Abbey. Even Simon, the wonderful priest who would visit us weekly when Anne was ill, had disappeared on his own journey to Ethiopia.

"Are you keeping busy, Dad?" Louisa asks.

"Sure. So many dinner parties, I can't keep up!" I joke.

It is only after I make the joke that I realise you rarely see single people at dinner parties. I will have to work hard to have any social contact at all from now on.

I travel to France to see Louisa in February. Anything for a change of scenery. My spending starts to spiral out of control. I am seduced by fine silks and fancy tailoring.

I think if I look good, perhaps I will start to feel good.

I have spent the last ten years looking after Anne, and really not paying much attention to myself. Of course I keep up with my exercise, that is always a constant, and always will be. The only thing that keeps me going are my visits to the gym at the Bath Spa Hotel three times a week. I crave the endorphins the exercise releases, and I believe it helps with easing my physical and mental suffering. Now I know it's the only reason I retain my sanity throughout the whole ordeal.

Louisa starts to make comments about my spending. I am indignant, but also at a loss as to what to say to her. On the one hand, I can spend my money any which way I please. On the other hand, I also understand at some level that the more I spend, the less happy I become.

I am powerless to control it.

"Dad, maybe you can take up a hobby or something when you get home," Louisa suggests gently.

I agree, of course. I just don't know what hobby to take up. I have lost faith in the Abbey, and I don't feel like becoming involved with it again just yet. I feel hurt and abandoned when I think about it. Anne's illness had been so isolating, and the love and support I thought would be there from the Abbey community didn't quite materialise. That's a subject for another day, but one that I think about a lot.

I return to Bath after my brief holiday in Meribel.

Bereft, adrift, directionless, my spending takes an unexpected turn. Gone are the small sums spent on clothes. I start to buy properties, cars, large ticket items. I travel to and buy houses in South Africa, Dorset, Spain. Galloping towards financial ruin, emotional distress and my near death.

Forty-Seven

Chris and Anne

1963

ANNE AND I DATED FOR TWO YEARS BEFORE I PROPOSED
to her. Memories of that time catch me unaware.

"Tell me a story," she used to say, on our long drives
down to Wales to visit her family.

I am so intoxicated with Anne, with her beauty
and intelligence, that I am always astonished that she is
interested in anything I have to say. I soon get over any
shyness, as Anne asks questions, shows such interest in my
life and my thoughts.

Memories of those drives come back to visit me often.

We are travelling down to visit her aunt and uncle one beautiful
summer morning, and our chatter has come to a halt.

As is customary, Anne asks me, "Tell me a story."

"What do you want to know?" I respond automatically.

"Anything. You are a natural storyteller. I notice it most when you meet my relatives. Always a good tale to tell. I just love listening to you talk," says Anne.

I sneak a quick look at her out of the side of my eye. Her radiant face is turned towards the open window, the summer sun glinting off her golden hair and lighting up her cornflower-blue eyes. The scenery beyond the window is almost as stunning as my girl. I want to pinch myself; I can't believe my luck.

Today, I decide I want to make her laugh.

I rack my brain.

"OK. So there was this one time, when I was working in the factory at Sharps Toffees in Maidstone—"

"Before you came down to Wiltshire?" Anne interrupts.

"Yes, then. I was very young and getting up at five in the morning to get to the factory for the 6am shift. I had a good routine. When I got to work, I often found myself gravitating towards this large chap. He had a mysterious sort of demeanour, which I liked. Craggy face, massive shoulders. Brooding. We used to work together, side by side. In silence, mostly. This went on like this for a few months. I would turn up for work. Sometimes he was there, sometimes he wasn't. If he was, he would step aside, and I would slot in, ready to work next to him for the eight-hour shift."

"He sounds odd," Anne says. "Was he mute?"

"No!" I snort, and carry on with my story.

"One day, this large, mysterious man says to me, out of the blue, 'Do you know what I do?' he asks. 'Make toffee?' I say back, watching him stirring the sugar that will turn into sticky sweets, same as we have been doing day in, day out for months. '*No!*' he boomed—"

"*Boomed*?" Anne interrupts again, with a teasing tone in her voice. "Why was he booming?"

"Well. I seem to remember him booming, but he probably spoke normally. But anyway, that's by the by. Stop interrupting. You will never guess what he said…" I continue.

"What? Come on, Chris, don't leave me in suspense. I can't imagine what he did. Clearly something interesting, or he wouldn't be 'booming' and you wouldn't be telling me this story."

"He was the deputy hangman to Pierrepoint, the last hangman in the UK. Making toffee on his days off, of all things."

"A real-life hangman? Someone to put the noose around the neck and swing the criminals, sort of hangman?"

"That's the one. There is even a street near the centre of Bath named after him. Pierrepoint Street. Anyway, this large man, he used to tell me all the stories, you know. I never had one dull day at work after he started to talk to me. He wouldn't talk to anyone else on the factory floor. He would search me out and we would stand side by side, stirring, drenched in the scent of burnt sugar, and he would tell me all these things. About what the criminals had done, what they said, even their last words."

"Urgh. Well, that makes me shudder. And I'm not sure I will enjoy a toffee quite as much in the future, knowing that. He might have made that toffee! The day after hanging a rotten criminal!" Anne exclaims, clutching her white knitted cardigan closer around her.

"Well, I don't think he made the toffee taste of 'criminal' just by stirring it. That would have been a skill indeed!"

"I still don't like the sound of it," Anne says.

"He was an ex-Cambridge graduate, a real clever sort of chap," I continue. "He realised fairly early on that he didn't want to go into academia, and somehow decided that the life of a hangman was for him! So off he went to Maidstone to fulfil his dream."

"What a macabre story."

"He was perfectly charming," I say. "The only unnerving thing was, sometimes he would be there, and sometimes he wasn't. And that's when I knew he was off, *doing a death*. When he came back in the next day, we would have a talk about who it was this time, and what they had done. The stories he would tell would raise the hairs on your neck."

Anne looks at me suspiciously.

"You're making this up. To impress me."

"I am certainly not," I say indignantly. "These are just the sort of things that happen to me. I couldn't dream someone like him up. He was just there."

"Well, don't tell Aunt Madeleine about him, that's all I'll say. I don't think her nerves would take it. It's like something out of a Dickens novel!" Anne says, leaning forward to turn up the radio.

We sing along to music for the remainder of the journey down to the Welsh coast, as happy as a courting couple learning stories about each other could be.

These are the conversations that flash up unexpectedly in the darkest of nights. Sometimes they make me laugh. Sometimes, they make me weep until I don't think I can cry anymore. That's the cruel nature of grief.

Forty-Eight

The Wilderness

2003–10

WHEN ANNE DIES, I FIND I CAN'T COME TO ANY decision on my own.

I have spent the last forty years being told what to do. I just hadn't realised it.

Anne was always decisive and certain of her opinions. She had steered us quietly through the long years of our marriage, taking care of everything quickly and without fuss. It was a quality I admired in Anne enormously. She was such a strong person. Now with Anne gone, I find it very difficult to focus. I feel devastated to be left.

There is no one to help me. Our friends have abandoned us. Bath Abbey has abandoned me. I don't want to burden Louisa. I am completely alone.

I don't know how to ask for help.

My life has been filled with grief and suffering for so long, I don't know who I am anymore. Days I used to spend travelling to Dorothy House, or attending to Anne, are now over.

My own sense of mortality starts playing on my mind. I have frailties in my shoulders, my legs, my bowels. I am adrift, high on morphine for the constant pain I am in. I feel completely cut off from my life.

I keep thinking back to the shock of her death. I knew she was going to die. I just didn't believe she would have the gall to actually do it.

I need a project to keep me busy. My life has been so structured with Anne. She was a stronger character than me, but I knew exactly what to do with my life before. Now I don't. It is a harsh realisation. To consider oneself as a strong person, and to find out that you are, in fact, not.

The worst thing is I know I am going off the rails. I just don't know how badly, and who to tell. I heard the other day that you should never make any life-changing decisions in the first months after a loved one's death. Your grief is bound to be too strong and your decisions unhinged. If only I had known this at the time. It might have prevented the months and years of heartache that were to come, as we shall see.

Forty-Nine

Chris

Selling Alpine Cottage 2004

"Hi, Louisa."

I can tell my voice is subdued. I can't help it. The decision I have made is huge.

"Hi, Dad." Louisa's tone matches mine.

She is low again today. Maybe what I say to her now will help cheer her up.

"I have decided to sell Alpine Cottage," I say, decisively.

"No!" Louisa gasps. "You can't sell the family home! You, me, Mum – we lived there for so many happy years!"

"I know, but…" I say, a little taken aback at the strength of her objection.

"Well…" Louisa takes a little pause. "I guess not so happy towards the end," she says, sighing. "It doesn't change the fact that all my childhood memories are tied up there, at Alpine Cottage. It's your safe haven! And mine."

I can tell she is very upset.

"Sorry, Louisa. I have made my decision. You are getting married and will need a place to live. I don't need this big house anymore, and it would be my honour to help you out a little bit. You know, financially. I can do that with the proceeds of the house. I'm sure I'll get a good price for it."

I pause and glance around my elegant living room, now equipment-free. It's back to how it was before Anne became ill and we had to modify everything. I remember the awful feeling of real deep depression I felt transforming Alpine Cottage from a makeshift nursing home into a proper home again. I think about the two hoists that hauled Anne from one end of the room to the other. Invaluable for getting her onto the commode or placing her in the special shower chair she used. When the room had been cleared, I had to return to a real life that was painful, with the realisation that my Anne had gone for good to another place. A place that none of us left on earth know about.

I look out of the large window overlooking Bath, and my heart gives a little lurch at the thought of not being able to enjoy this wonderful view in the future.

"Anyway, I've had enough of city life," I say cheerfully. "I fancy a bit of sea air. I am looking to move to the Dorset coast. A change of scene is exactly what I need."

Louisa is very quiet.

"Well, Dad," she says after a while. "Your money is your money. You can do what you like with it. And of course I would be silly not to accept your very generous offer of helping me and Andrew onto the housing ladder. I just want to know that you have thought about it."

"Of course I have thought about it, Louisa. It's a big decision, but one that I think is right."

We chat for a bit and I hang up the receiver. I have no idea if it's right or not. All I know is that I don't know what to do. Now Anne isn't here. And a change is as good as rest, as they say.

Fifty

The Spanish Dream

Spring 2003

LOOKING BACK, THE DECISION TO SELL ALPINE Cottage is the snowball that rolls out of control and starts an avalanche of disaster.

Selling up and moving to Dorset is the start of a period of seven years that nearly ends in tragedy. At the time I had no concept of the impact my rash decisions would have, but sadly there is no one around to advise me. More importantly, there is no one around to stop me doing what I like.

And I like to spend money.

Doing whatever I want to, after a lifetime considering the feelings of Anne or others, is terrifying and exhilarating at the same time. I become addicted to the thrill of it.

It starts here. The first decision of many that takes me down the path to financial and emotional ruin.

I take a walk down Milsom Street in Bath, one lovely afternoon in spring. I ponder the points that have arisen during my recent meeting with the solicitor to discuss Anne's will.

It's at this meeting that I decide to sell Alpine Cottage on an impulse. Anne would have wanted to help Louisa out with her first home, and I am looking for a fresh start. It seems the perfect solution.

I am financially stable for the first time in my life. My assets on paper means I am now a millionaire. I'm a bachelor able to spend and do whatever I want, whenever I want.

I am distracted by a large sign in a window in a Georgian shopfront at the bottom of the hill.

"The Spanish Dream!"

The letters are large, superimposed over a stunning image of a white-washed villa overlooking the Mediterranean Sea.

I don't know what makes me stop and look more closely. I conjure up visions of living in an exotic Spanish villa, when suddenly I realise I am being smiled at by a very attractive lady on the other side of the window. I am flustered at being observed.

Not knowing what to do, I decide to walk slowly to the door and push it open.

"Hello." She smiles at me.

"Hello." I smile back. "The Spanish Dream, hey? Sounds pretty good to me," I say, chuckling nervously.

The lady pushes her chair back and offers her hand in greeting.

"Kirsty."

"Chris," I mumble back, suddenly aware it's been a while since I've interacted with anyone as beautiful as Kirsty.

So consumed with my grief, I sleepwalk through daily life. Not today.

I suddenly feel a buzzing in my body.

It's excitement.

It's the feeling I get before I'm about to spend a large amount of money.

Oh, how I now wish I had listened to that buzz and recognised it for the warning sign it was.

Kirsty rolls her chair back and deftly plucks out a brochure from the filing cabinet behind her.

"Does this look dreamy to you?" she asks, placing the glossy pages in front of me.

I stare transfixed at idyllic illustrations of luxurious marble villas, landscaped gardens and swimming pools glittering under the cloudless blue skies.

"Well, yes," I admit, flicking through page upon page of apartment plans and house specifications. "Where is this?"

"Our properties are situated in an area along the Costa del Sol coastline. Stunning. These properties are currently under construction and yours to buy today at an incredible price."

I am listening, but not paying much attention.

"So, how much would a three-bedroom apartment cost me?" I ask, my eyes drawn to a particularly attractive photograph.

"As little as £175,000," Kirsty purrs, "and better still – a four-bedroom town house could be yours for the frankly ludicrous price of £250,000! A complete steal!"

To be honest, I have no idea whether it's a complete steal or not.

Remember, I have just wandered into Kirsty's office off the street on a whim and have no knowledge of the Spanish property market.

Now I find myself clutching a brochure and seriously contemplating buying a villa in sunny Spain.

The sensible part of my brain kicks in.

What a fool you are! I say to myself.

I put the brochure back down on the table, smile apologetically, and start to rise out of the chair.

"Well, thank you very much…" I say.

"You also might be interested to know that there is a guaranteed rental income and a fifty per cent mortgage offer…"

Kirsty knows what she's doing. Her smile when I sit back down tells me that she has done this before. I am helpless in the face of such ruthless yet charming salesmanship.

"OK. You've got me. Tell me more…" I ask.

She tells me a lot. About the exceptional value, the quality of life, the incredible investment. What she doesn't tell me are details that prove my undoing down the line. That the rental scheme terms includes the purchase of an expensive furniture package from the company, substantially adding to the costs; that sort of thing.

"If you are interested, and forgive me, but I think you are…" Kirsty flashes me that killer smile again.

I shrug in response, trying to play it cool, but lean forward to hear more.

"…why don't you allow me to fly you to the Costa del Sol to check out the area? All expenses paid, it goes without saying. A nice long weekend away, so you can see for yourself what an irresistible opportunity this is. You, and, of course, your partner?" she enquires with a raised eyebrow.

"No, no partner." I laugh, a bit sadly.

"Oh! That does surprise me!"

Is she flirting with me? I feel flattered.

"My wife died six months ago. I could bring my daughter, though, I know she might be pleased of a little break."

As I say this, I suddenly realise that I have just committed to going to Marbella, and that I am going with the view to buying a property abroad.

Hats off to Kirsty – she is a truly impressive salesperson.

I only popped out for a stroll and to pick up some supper.

Fifty-One

Spain

Summer 2003

"Louisa, fancy a trip to the Costa del Sol? Bit of sunshine, time together with your old dad?"

"Well, that sounds exciting. What's brought this on?"

"Just a little whim. I think you need a treat. Indulge me, daughter."

I hang up, pleased that Louisa has agreed to accompany me on my trip. I don't dwell on the fact that she doesn't know the full story or the real reason why we are going. She will know soon enough.

We travel up the mountain above Estepona in a luxury air-conditioned coach. We can see Morocco in the distance across the Mediterranean Sea, and the excitement in the coach is at fever pitch. Kirsty tells us that we will shortly arrive at the Duquesa development.

We peer as if we can see it, our imaginations running away with us.

The show house is indeed impressive. We enter the complex through an archway that frames an exotic courtyard filled with the green of palm trees, flashes of red and pink and yellow of bougainvillea, mimosa and hibiscus. An infinity pool surrounded by loungers looks enticing in the summer heat.

"Your houses and apartments will all be finished to the same exacting standards and specifications," Kirsty explains as she gives us a guided tour around the show home.

"Marble floors, air conditioning, granite worktop surfaces, integrated kitchen units and communal pool. Everything is included in the price. I don't need to tell you, it's a complete bargain when you see what you're getting."

I look at my fellow passengers and feel a pang of anxiety. They are all here to buy. What if I miss out on my opportunity?

I glance at Louisa. She doesn't seem upset to be here, in fact she seems as excited as the others. I made the right call not telling her the real reason we are here before we made the trip out. She would have tried to talk me out of it.

Kirsty is speaking again. I turn to her and pay attention.

"What would you, as buyers, be interested in, I ask myself?" Kirsty closes her eyes and sweeps her arms at us theatrically.

"I imagine your thoughts are revolving round the investment potential, capital appreciation and rental returns, am I right? Well, I have looked into that for you guys already. The great news is that prices are likely to increase by at least twenty per cent in the next few months."

My fellow passengers gasp and murmur, and I nod at them with a big grin. The mood is infectious.

"Well, that's what happens when supply exceeds demand! We also know the pound is strong against the euro, so this really is a no-brainer," Kirsty says, triumphantly.

"I have personally reserved three properties," she continues. "An apartment here at the Duquesa development, for my parents, a town house in Estrella, and another on the Mijas site."

Kirsty is on a roll; she continues to wave her arms excitedly about her three investments. It's mesmeric.

Kirsty is interrupted. A man has stepped forward and cut her off.

"What about the rumour I've heard? Apparently the town hall officials are being prosecuted for granting illegal building licences?"

We all peer round to see who is talking. He is being a bit of a buzzkill.

The small man starts listing all the things he has concerns about.

I wish now I had listened more carefully.

"…furnishing, seven per cent Spanish income tax, solicitor fees, local taxes. What about Ring Bull Properties? We don't know anything about you. Would you be willing to show us copies of your annual accounts?"

Kirsty looks affronted, and opens her mouth to respond, but the small man continues.

"Also – how do we know that our shiny new villas won't be bulldozed to the ground if it turns out that the land was purchased illegally by the parties involved? Do you or Ring Bull Properties guarantee to protect our money if you, or the developer, go bust?"

Kirsty raised her hand in a reassuring manner.

"Don't fret… Tim, is it? I have just told you that I have personally invested nearly one million euros in properties here. Do you think I would have done that if I had any concerns?"

She flashes us that mesmerising smile again.

"The operations director will answer any further questions tonight."

And with that, she directs us back onto the buses to visit the potential sites.

Louisa is very quiet next to me as we bump along the mountain roads.

"What do you think, Louisa? Exciting?" I whisper, trying to quell my own anxieties.

"Hmm." Her answer is non-committal.

I don't push it and stare out the window at the approaching coastline.

The new complex is built into the hillside. Luxury villas, owned mainly by German millionaires, look down over the plot towards the sea.

"Wow, check out that view!" I exclaim as we alight

from the coach.

Louisa does seem a little more enthusiastic. It's hard not to be charmed.

"Well, it has great views, fabulous location. I can imagine it would be a great holiday destination for your visiting grandchildren!" she says with a smile, the first time I have heard her chuckle today.

Tim, our resident killjoy, steps forward.

"Kirsty. This is all very nice. Are you sure the planners – or indeed, the owners of those villas – would allow the development of an apartment block that would seriously impair their view? How do we know that Mijas Town Hall will give final approval to this development and grant the habitation licence?"

I am getting a little tired of Tim.

As is Kirsty, I notice. I push his valid questions to the back of my mind, again.

Kirsty smiles at Tim, holds up one finger in apology, and takes a phone call. She talks animatedly into the mouthpiece as we watch. When she turns back to us, she gives a big shrug.

"OK, Tim, so here's the thing. I would have suggested you direct your *numerous* questions to our operations director – but as it turns out, it is of no consequence anymore."

Tim looks confused.

"Why?" he asks.

Kirsty ignores him. She shakes her head sadly and turns to me.

"I'm so sorry, Chris. Head office have just called to confirm that all these plots are reserved. I know you were particularly keen on plot 10."

The disappointment I feel is almost overwhelming. Even Louisa looks downcast.

Tim shrugs, pats me on the shoulder and says, "Sounds like you dodged a bullet!"

Kirsty's phone rings again. She turns and walks away from the group.

"Wow!" Her voice rings out.

Kirsty looks excited as she races up to me.

"It must be your lucky day. Plot number 10 is back up for sale! The current owner just called; she's unable to proceed with her purchase. It's yours if you want it."

I cannot believe my luck. I stare at Kirsty with my mouth open.

"I don't want to rush you, but we will be relisting plot 10 on our website immediately. Unless you tell me right now you are interested, of course. £250,000 and it's yours. Plus legal costs of £10,000 and a £5,000 reservation fee payable on signing the contract. I'm sure I don't need to tell you. This is a once-in-a-lifetime opportunity…"

Kirsty raises her eyebrow at me, finger poised over her mobile phone as if she is about to call to confirm the purchase, then and there.

I look at her, and my mind is a whirr.

I already know I'm going to proceed.

"I will get back to you as soon as I've spoken to my financial advisor," I inform Kirsty, trying not to sound too eager. "Please let me know if anyone else expresses any interest in the meantime."

Kirsty slips her mobile into her handbag and tilts her head.

"Your call, Chris. You can see that it's a very desirable plot. I will leave you to talk to your financial advisor…"

Kirsty glances at Louisa. She can tell Louisa stands between me and her commission.

"…and daughter, of course."

And with that she walks off to join the group making their way back to the bus.

I feel sick with the excitement, anxiety and worry that I will lose the plot. I realise it's the first time in six months I haven't thought of Anne.

I turn and clutch Louisa.

"It's meant to be, darling! What luck!"

"Yes, Dad," Louisa answers. "Luck indeed…"

Fifty-Two

Am I Bipolar?

2010

LOUISA AND I ARE TAKING A RARE WALK BY THE canal. It's a beautiful summer evening, the houses around us glowing in the fading rays. We have been walking in silence for some ten minutes or so, and I am delighted to be walking with my daughter. Doing something normal, something that feels comfortable.

"Dad, your spending…" Louisa starts.

"Mmhmm," I mumble. I feel my shoulders tense straight away.

"I have been looking it up, online. The way you spend… it doesn't feel right."

Oh. She had to go and ruin it, didn't she?

Louisa is trying to broach the subject in her usual kind way.

She takes after her mother, I think fondly, trying to

quell the rising irritation that she is bringing the subject up. Yet again. Bossy and determined. Always kind.

"Louisa, it's fine," I say. "I'm just enjoying myself. Surely you want your old dad to have a bit of fun? It's all been a bit tricky for so long."

I know that I am lying to her, and also to myself.

My spending is not fine. It hasn't been fine for a while.

I have started pushing my credit card bills to the back of the writing bureau. They are mounting up, unopened.

Terrifying, both in amount and physical quantity.

I saw Louisa cast a questioning eye over the unopened post the other day when she had come round for tea with Andrew. I was annoyed with myself for not having hidden the letters more thoroughly, from her and from myself.

Louisa had just looked at me with a raised eyebrow but hadn't said anything.

I thought I had got away with it. Clearly not.

"Could… could you have some sort of bipolar disorder, Dad? A type of manic depression? You have been through so much in your life. It wouldn't be unreasonable to look into the possibility…"

Louisa is stuttering. However kindly she says it, it makes no difference.

I feel like someone has hit me in the stomach.

Bipolar? *That's a serious mental illness*, I think to myself. One that requires medication and management. A bipolar diagnosis goes against everything that I think I am. Measured and in control.

I stop walking for a minute. I pretend to do up the lace on my walking boot. I have my head bent so Louisa can't see the expression on my face. I am moving through many emotions.

Shock, then doubt, then anger.

"How dare you?" I say coldly and quietly.

"Pardon?" Louisa crouches to hear me more clearly.

"Of course I'm not bipolar."

"Have bipolar disorder, you mean," Louisa says automatically, standing up again. She is very good at saying things as they are. No room for ambiguity. Like her mother.

"Whatever. Either way, I don't have it!"

Louisa takes my hand, which I know is shaking. I never raise my voice. I can tell from her face she is regretting raising the subject.

"Dad. OK. OK. It's just something to consider. I don't think you feel very good right now, and something needs to be done about your spending. It feels out of control. *You* feel out of control. I just want you to think about going to see someone, that's all."

Louisa rises and gives me a kiss on the cheek, lifts my sunglasses and looks into my eyes. I squint back at her against the dropping sun.

"Come on," she says. "We've done enough walking. Let's go and get that cream tea we promised ourselves. A good treat after our afternoon exertions."

Louisa smiles broadly at me, willing forgiveness. And off we walk to our favourite tea house, subject closed, trying to rekindle the easy companionship we had enjoyed just ten minutes earlier.

Fifty-Three

Psychiatrist

2010

I CAN'T GET IT OUT OF MY MIND.

A day later, I have made an appointment with the psychiatrist.

"Tell me how you feel," he says.

My psychiatrist is a brusque, no-nonsense sort of man. I like him very much.

"*I'm fine, thanks*. It's my daughter that tells me I'm not. She thinks I spend too much money, and that I am out of control," I say.

I laugh amiably, rolling my eyes as if the suggestion is ludicrous.

The suggestion isn't off the mark at all. It's a permanent worry. *This psychiatrist doesn't need to know that*, I tell myself.

"She thinks…" I lean forward and lower my voice, "… that I am bipolar! Sorry, let me correct that. She believes

I have bipolar disorder, manic depression. Whatever you want to call it."

The psychiatrist stops taking notes and looks at me.

"And what do you think?" he asks, with genuine interest.

"Of course not! Of course I don't."

I know I am behaving defensively, but I know how I feel.

"My wife died," I continue. "It was hard. I had to look after her for a long time. She had Friedreich's Ataxia."

My psychiatrist murmurs in sympathy. I'm impressed he knows what it is.

"It was awful," I continue. "Watching someone you love, die in front of you like that. No cure, no remedy. Ten years! It has taken its toll, emotionally, physically. And yes, financially."

I take a breath.

The psychiatrist has stopped taking notes; he is looking at me. I shall have to tread carefully, get my composure back.

"I'm not going to lie. I do feel upset sometimes. A lot of the time, even."

I am working hard to keep the wobble in my voice in check. It wouldn't do to have a breakdown here, in this man's office. He would have me locked up.

The psychiatrist nods. He taps his pen against the notes in front of him. When he speaks, his tone is matter-of-fact.

"Of course. I understand. It's going to take a toll on anyone, caring for a terminally ill patient. Grief is a funny thing. Maybe you did need to buy some new things, treat yourself a little. To confront a new chapter in your life feeling something different. I imagine looking good, taking care of yourself, was pretty low on your list? You know, when you were in the thick of caring for Anne?" He looks at me questioningly through his thick grey eyebrows.

I nod.

The psychiatrist sighs. "Look. See how you go. I think that from what you've told me, I see no reason to start treatment for a bipolar diagnosis."

"So… no lithium?" I say in relief. It was the main thing I was worried about. I had heard and read dreadful things about the side effects of taking the medication.

"No lithium," the psychiatrist says, with a smile. "However," he continues, scribbling something on his prescription pad. "I do think that it would be a good idea to up the dose of your current antidepressant medication and also I can recommend a good therapist. It would do you good to have someone to speak to. Get all this off your chest."

Fifty-Four

New Therapist Lucy

2010-11

I START SEEING LUCY, THE RECOMMENDED THERAPIST. I am surprised to find out that she is the estate agent that sold Alpine Cottage.

"I retrained," she explains, after I point out that we have met before. "Will it be a problem, do you think?"

"Not in the slightest," I reply.

Maybe this won't be awful. In truth, I am delighted, as I had found her very warm and compassionate as an estate agent, and she proves just as warm as a therapist.

I see her once a week and start to look forward to our regular visits. We mainly discuss Anne, but we also touch on subjects that prove almost as difficult, if not more.

"We have talked a lot about your feelings over the past months," Lucy says today, having settled on the chair in front of me.

"It's coming up to a year!" I say. I can't quite believe it myself. The time has flown by.

"How do you think it's going?" Lucy asks.

"I think it's going well." A doubt creeps in. "Don't you?" I ask.

"Absolutely," Lucy says, reassuringly. "I think we discussed that this would be our last session. I just wanted to make sure you feel it's the right time."

I think about it. I shall miss my weekly sessions, they have become a bit of a lifeline.

"Well, I don't really know how I'm going to move forward without you. It does make me nervous. But it's probably time, as you say."

"We've covered a lot of ground," Lucy says. "I think you've come a long way," she continues. "We have spoken frankly about your wife, her death, the impact on your mental health having to come to terms with such a traumatic experience. I think the gaps we, or more importantly you, now must fill are the following. You need to explore the reasons why you embarked on such self-destructive behaviour after Anne's death. Particularly in your behaviour towards Julie."

Lucy sits back and waits for me to speak.

My mouth is dry. This is the one topic I don't really want to discuss.

"Well, what would you like me to talk about today?" I say, stalling for time.

"Let's start from the beginning, maybe. Why did you decide to start a relationship with Julie? You were barely nine months into mourning your wife's death, is that right?"

Do I hear judgement in her voice? I hope not. Admittedly nine months is not a long time to embark on a new relationship after your wife of thirty-seven years has passed away. I remind myself that I had been in mourning for a lot longer than that. I had started my mourning the day of Anne's terminal diagnosis. I decide to give Lucy the benefit of the doubt and answer neutrally.

"I saw Julie as a potential partner. A soulmate, to replace my irreplaceable Anne. I guess that's where the problem lay." I smile ruefully.

"Was it a successful relationship?" Lucy asks.

"No. I wouldn't say that. Particularly in the way it ended," I say, regretfully.

"It's normal for men who suffer depression, especially for long periods of time, to feel like this."

Lucy looks around her bright office in search of the right words.

"Would it be fair to say you became obsessed with her in your search for warmth and affection and friendship? This would create the perfect conditions for a rebound scenario. You could have easily confused your search for connection with real love, do you think that's possible?"

I nod and put my head in my hands. I stare at the grey squares etched into the carpet. I had been so unfair to Julie. I could see that now. Particularly as she had been searching for something to heal her own broken heart. Maybe it was inevitable the relationship didn't flourish under those conditions.

"Please can I have another glass of water?" I ask. My

mouth is dry and my tongue is sticking to the roof of my mouth. Even my body doesn't want to talk about this.

Lucy stands and pours me a large glass of water from the jug she keeps on her desk. She pours one for herself and comes and sits down again, handing me my water.

I focus on the coolness of the glass in my hands as I try and think of the best way to explain.

"The thing is. Julie wasn't... isn't... a bad person. I don't think I'm a bad person either. But for some reason we just didn't bring out the best in each other."

Lucy nods, her face encouraging me.

"What do you mean by that?"

"Well, Julie was right in some of her observations. I had become self-obsessed. Everything I did, wanted to do, was to satisfy my own urges, wants and desires. She needed to end the relationship. I wasn't the person I thought I was. Or wanted to be."

"I was lucky," I continue. "My relationship with Julie was over, and I was able to sell my property in Spain before the market crashed in 2008."

"And that was when you came back to Bath?" Lucy asks.

"Yes. I knew I wanted to return home, to get back to Louisa."

"And that's where you are now, more stable, more secure."

"Yes, thanks to your help." I smile gratefully.

Lucy will never know just how much she has helped me.

"You are a strong person, Chris," Lucy says gently.

I am reminded of Anne's words, all those years ago, when she said the same thing. I shrug sadly.

"Stronger than you know," Lucy continues. "You have the ability to make and maintain strong friendships and relationships. Don't view your relationship with Julie as a failure. Take it as a springboard from which you will have other more meaningful interactions. Go forth and live your life. You have all the tools now."

Lucy smiles at me.

I smile back. I wish I had the strength of her conviction.

"Thank you. From the bottom of my heart. I wouldn't be here without you," I say, sincerely.

Fifty-Five

Julie

September 2003

I MEET JULIE ON A BLIND DATE.

She is warm and kind, and I am a lost soul.

Anne was right. I am finding it very difficult to cope on my own. Julie has just come out of a very destructive marriage, and so we are both lost together, trying to steer our way through the tricky waters of grief.

"Tell me about your time in South Africa. You talk of it often, and I think you should return and visit. Nothing is stopping you now, is it?"

"No" I respond.

Julie and I have been dating for a few weeks now, and I am not sure how much to open up to her about the difficult relationship I had with my mother. I have been thinking of her since Anne died, craving the warmth of a motherly figure.

"Since the age of twelve, when I was packed off to live with my father, I have always thought I would return to South Africa and be near my mother again."

"But why? Didn't you resent her? Dare I say it – hate her a little for doing that to you? Sending you away like that when you were just a little boy?"

Julie senses she's treading on thin ice, and she places her hand over mine reassuringly.

I jump a little at the cool smoothness of her palm but then relax. It's not unpleasant, and I realise it's the first time a woman has touched me since Anne.

I take a while to answer and look off over the harbour. We are having a drink by the coast and the sea air is making me feel nostalgic.

"Well. My father certainly didn't want me to ever return to South Africa. He was very clear about that. But as I grew older, I started to understand that actually my mother made a great sacrifice sending me away. It must have hurt her as much as it hurt me. She had no choice, really."

I pinch the bridge of my nose. I'm starting to feel emotional. It is always so hard to talk about this period of my life. I had adored my mother so much, and she had discarded me as if I were of no import. Her decision had affected every future relationship of mine. I wonder if she had any idea what she had done.

Julie looks at me, carries on stroking my hand.

"Why do you say she had no choice?"

"Well, she married a terrible man. His name was Tom. He exerted too much influence over her, who knows why.

And, the truth of it is, she was weak in the face of his wishes." I swallow down my anger at the memory of Tom.

"His first demand when he got together with my mother was that I be gone. Completely off the scene."

I laugh dryly.

"He certainly achieved that. I couldn't have been sent much further away than England, could I?"

Julie raises one corner of her mouth in a half-smile.

"How did you feel about it at the time?" she asks.

I am starting to feel uncomfortable about the line of questioning. It is a subject I keep close to my heart, and I have shared it with very few people.

I decide to take the plunge. If I can't trust Julie, who can I trust?

"A mixture of things. Tom was an alcoholic and a bully. He ruled my mother and her emotions with an iron fist. I was too young to understand any of this, of course. But looking back on it, I just wish I had been a bit older, wiser and able to stand up for her a bit more. Not that she would have wanted me to. She couldn't see what was happening under her very nose."

"Did anyone else know he was like this?" Julie is intrigued now.

I laugh again.

"Well, put it this way. His two children from his first marriage disowned him, because of his appalling behaviour towards my mother! Not even their own mother – mine! That should give you some idea of his awful personality."

I can't help it, but just the memory of my mother's kindness, and the terrible sacrifice she had to make, affecting all around her, causes a tear to squeeze from the corner of my eye.

Julie is quiet for a long time.

"It must have been very hard for you, Chris. I can't imagine how such rejection at a young age has affected you."

I look at her. I decide not to tell her that I had grown up deeply unhappy, most likely depressed as a result of my mother's decision to send me to England to live with my father. I had been wrenched from the most idyllic childhood, from a mother I loved, childhood friends, and the warmth and freedom of South African childhood. Being forced to live in a cold, grey farmhouse with a cold, grey, unemotional father was the worst thing that could have happened to me.

"Anne changed all that for me," I say, quietly. I don't really want to bring her up, here in this romantic setting with another woman, but Anne is never far from my thoughts.

Fifty-Six

Financial Investments

2008

THE WORST TIME OF MY LIFE IS WHEN I AM NEARLY BROUGHT to ruin.

My financial advisor Steve, despite knowing that I am in shock and grief, decides to start playing around with my investments. The year is 2008. I have bought and sold the property in Spain by this point. Luckily, I sold up before the big crash.

I wander around my house in Dorset aimlessly. I don't know what to do. I am bored again, a dangerous state. I decide to call Steve for some advice.

I sit at my desk, pick up the telephone and tap in his number.

"Steve, how are you?"

"Good, Chris, good. What can I do for you?"

"Well, Steve, as you know, I have just sold my villa in Spain."

"Good time to sell!" Steve sounds buoyant, energised by my news.

"I'm obviously pleased that the currency exchange of the euro and the pound is in the pound's favour. I would like to reinvest the profit I made from the sale of the Spanish house. What should I do?"

Steve answers almost before I stop speaking. "This is great news, Chris! I have the perfect idea for your money. Let's put it into the derivatives market."

"Well, I'm not sure about that, it's not an area I'm particularly comfortable with," I start to say.

"Don't you worry, Chris. That's what I'm for. I know all about it. I tell you, the rewards can be huge."

Steve is so enthusiastic, I can't help being swept along with it.

Looking back, I was foolish to take him at face value. I should have done my own research, but I had no idea what I was doing.

When the call comes a few months later, it is a huge shock.

"I'm sorry." Steve's voice is certainly not buoyant now.

"Sorry? What about?" I ask, nervously.

"It would seem that the derivatives market was probably not the best place to put your savings at this time."

I twirl the cord on my phone and try and process what Steve is saying. Of course I had been keeping up with the news. It just hadn't occurred to me that it would directly affect me. It all sounded very shocking, the banking crisis and financial crash. But all the talk was centred around the impact for bankers. Not an average Joe Blogs like me.

Keep calm, I tell myself. I have always trusted Steve. Surely he has safeguarded my savings.

"As I always tell you, your investments can go down as well as up," Steve continues. "Derivatives in particular has proven very dicey."

I have a bad feeling.

"Well, which are they? Down or up?" I ask. I am daring him to spell it out.

"Umm. They are down. Very down. I'm sorry to say you have lost a lot on your current investments. There… there's not much left in the pot."

I am not sure what to say, so I ask him to send me the paperwork. I will have to see in black and white the extent of my losses. It all feels too much to process on top of the grief that I am having to deal with.

I later find out that Steve's firm also goes under. His poor advice had obviously had an impact on everyone involved, including himself.

I am in complete denial from this point on. Denial about my catastrophic financial situation, denial about the feelings I have for Julie in Dorset, denial about the overwhelming depression that is threatening to overtake me.

So I just go on as before.

I continue to buy houses, to be in a relationship, to grieve without acknowledging it. It is a very tricky state of mind to be in.

Fifty-Seven

Dorchester and Teeth Grinding ENT Specialist

2009

LOOKING BACK, OF COURSE I HAD DEPRESSION. IT'S obvious now. It wasn't so clear then. Back when I was in the thick of it.

"I think it might rain later," Julie says.

We are sitting at the cafe at the beach. It's a beautiful late summer day. The sky has been a brilliant blue all day, but now large grey clouds are starting to roll in over the bay.

"Do you think it might rain? Maybe we should head back before it does."

Julie looks at me.

I am clutching the side of my head.

"What is it, Chris?" Julie leans over the table and rubs my temple in concern.

"Nothing – I don't think. Maybe the drop in pressure is causing my head to ache," I say.

I stir my tea, take a sip. I pick up a cream- and jam-laden scone. I watch the seagulls screech over the pebbles. The waves break hard on the shore, picking up with the wind. A few families shiver behind their windbreakers. It might be late summer, but Julie is right. The temperature has dropped.

I bite into the scone. Suddenly, my head feels like it has been set on fire.

I give a small scream and drop the scone back on the plate.

Julie is alarmed. She leaps up to come and sit next to me on the wooden picnic bench.

"What's happening?" she asks in panic.

I am still clutching the side of my head.

"I… I don't know!" I moan. "Everything hurts!"

Excruciating pain radiates out over my cheek and ear. It spreads down my neck.

"Oh, Chris. I hope you aren't having a stroke. Or a heart attack," Julie says, anxiously.

"No, no. I don't think so. I have been having these pains on and off for a while," I reassure her, trying to breathe through the shooting pains.

I am not feeling that calm myself, so I find it difficult to convince Julie all is well. The pain is intense.

We pack up, scones abandoned on the brown melamine trays. We walk up the dusty path to the car park. As we drive up the hill, the first drops of rain start to fall. My head continues to ache, and I am pleased to be heading home back to Dorchester to a dark room and a large dose of painkillers.

I see the dentist, and then the doctor. They are both baffled.

"We have done all the possible tests. X-rays, ECGs, blood. You name it. Nothing is showing up," they say, puzzled.

"What should I do?" I ask.

"It might be nerve pain," they conclude. Nothing to be done.

I can't do nothing. That's what they told Anne and look where that ended up.

I go to the ENT specialist.

I am thoroughly examined, and he listens sympathetically.

Towards the end of the appointment, I have resigned myself to the fact he will also send me away with an unexplained diagnosis.

"Tell me what's going on in your life," the ENT specialist asks unexpectedly. Kindly.

"Well, my wife died. I don't know what I'm doing or who I am anymore," I say glumly.

I don't know what makes me open up to this man.

"Well, then I think it's highly likely you have depression, bearing in mind all you've gone through."

"No, no, I'm fine, thanks," I say doubtfully.

"These symptoms you describe to me. I see them in patients who are dealing with extreme grief. And, sometimes with depression. And often both at the same time. It's all part of it. Your body reacts to emotional events in unusual ways. It's cleverer than we are, in a way. Your physical pain is trying to tell you something."

I feel like I'm going to burst into tears in his office.

"So, what can I do? The pain is too much to bear. I can't just live with it," I say.

"How bad is it?"

"It's affecting everything," I say. "I love concerts. I can't stay to watch them anymore. I have terrible drumming in my ears if I listen to any loud noise. A constant humming noise, all the time. I can't go friends' houses. I can't stay out late past nine, because of the humming. It's exhausting. Impossible to live with."

"I suspect you are grinding your teeth with the stress."

I look at him.

"Surely I would notice?" I ask.

"Lots of people don't."

"When am I doing it?"

"At night, but possibly during the day too. I will get a mouth guard made up for you. Wear it day and night. Hopefully it will stop the teeth clenching and the trigeminal nerves being irritated. The pain should settle."

I leave his office, pleased to have a plan but anxious about what he's told me. If my undiagnosed depression is causing such intense physical pain, what else is it making me do?

Fifty-Eight

Complicated Feelings About My Relationship with Julie

2003–08

I HAVE ALWAYS HAD COMPLICATED FEELINGS ABOUT the physical nature of relationships. I am sent to a strict single-sex boarding school after I leave South Africa all those years ago, where I develop a deep Christian faith. With those teachings, comes the belief that there is no sex before marriage.

As a result of this upbringing, after Anne dies, I am torn between needing physical affection and wanting to uphold the fundamental teachings of my faith.

I justify starting up a relationship with Julie with the thought that perhaps here is someone that I could marry.

The premise of the relationship is not good because of this. I know I am still grieving for Anne and that I don't want to marry Julie. I also crave contact. I am so torn it causes a lot of issues.

"Did you know?" I say cheerfully to Julie one day, looking up from my newspaper.

"Did I know what?" Julie asks, turning to look at me. She is holding a wooden spatula aloft, tomato sauce dripping onto the quarry tiles in front of the stove. We are having spaghetti bolognese tonight. Julie is a good cook and I am so grateful for the wonderful home-cooked meals I am now enjoying after so many months of eating ready meals on my lap.

"Men often launch themselves into another relationship in a very short space of time after they have lost their loved ones."

Julie turns back to her pot and continues stirring.

"Is it in the newspaper?" she asks.

"Oh." I look down at the paper in my hand. I realise I have been staring at it for half an hour now but haven't read a single word. I haven't been able to concentrate on anything for months now, but I like to pretend that I am. "No, actually. I was just thinking about it."

"So, where did you hear that?" she asks.

"At my bereavement counselling session."

"I'm not shocked. Of course women are better at being on their own," Julie says lightly. "Like most things!"

I laugh and walk over to her and put my arms about her waist. I inhale the aromas of oregano and garlic. I'm starving.

"Do you think we got together too soon?" she asks. "After Anne, I mean?"

I know she can feel me freeze.

"Of course not," I answer.

I spin her round to look at me.

"That's not why I told you about it," I say.

She looks at me.

"Why, then? What reason?" she asks.

"Just thought it was an interesting fact," I say, feeling flustered. This was not the way I wanted the evening to go.

"I don't understand you sometimes, Chris. If that's not the reason, then I want you to think about why you told me."

Julie goes back to stirring her pot. I walk back to my armchair to blankly stare at my newspaper.

Why did I tell her? I seem to have a cruel streak in me these days. I now realise that what I said was inconsiderate. I was just thinking about myself again. I had been quite interested in the statistic when the counsellor had mentioned it earlier today. Why on earth I thought it was appropriate to share with the person I had got together with after my bereavement I don't know.

"After death, the person left behind can feel very alone," the counsellor had said. "Their need for support, for someone to care for them, can feel overwhelming. So often, they get together with the wrong person for the wrong reasons."

This resonated with me. I was going against my whole ethical standpoint, having a relationship outside of marriage. It wasn't the right thing to do, and it wasn't the right person to do it with.

I have come to realise that only today.

I have a lot of thinking to do.

Fifty-Nine

Escaping from Grief

Bath, 2008

Looking back, my relationship with Julie was part of my journey to try and escape my grief.

"Dad, are you sure you are doing the right thing? With Julie? I'm happy that you are in a relationship, don't get me wrong," Louisa says one day. "It just all feels very fast."

Louisa is right, of course. It is very fast.

We are having lunch at her house. I look around at the cosy kitchen, the toys strewn on the floor. I feel so safe and warm here. I experience a rush of gladness that I was able to help her buy this home. Even though it meant the sale of Alpine Cottage, it was the right thing to do. She deserves it after everything.

Louisa sets down a big salad on the pine table and picks up a discarded sippy cup of juice. She dangles it from one finger as she looks down at me.

"I like Julie very much, you know I do. I am just concerned that you don't seem as happy as you should be."

I sit there and play with my fork.

"I'm fine, Louisa. Really. Julie and I are fine."

I know that Louisa is correct about this too. I am not fine, and my relationship with Julie is not good. Why do I always say, "I'm fine, thanks?" when I'm hiding behind a mask, unable to open up and admit I have a problem.

"Well, all I'm saying, Dad, is that if you want to come back to Bath, I would like it very much."

Louisa kisses the top of my head and puts the sippy cup by the sink.

We sit down to eat.

"Don't you miss the Abbey? Your singing?" Louisa asks in between mouthfuls of pasta.

"Of course. It does feel a bit awkward, though. Some of my old friends from the Abbey have made comments about me."

"What do you mean?" Louisa grinds some pepper over her plate and offers it to me.

I accept it.

"They have said that I've changed. That I am a completely different person." I pause. "Do you think I'm a completely different person? Since Mum died?"

Louisa sighs and puts her fork down.

"You have brought me up to be truthful, so I won't change that now. Yes, you have changed a bit. It's natural. You lost Mum, you moved to a different part of the country. Everything you knew was turned upside down.

No wonder you seem a bit… out of sorts." Louisa picks up her fork and starts eating again.

"Out of sorts?" I am intrigued.

"Yes. Different to how you were before." Louisa pauses. "Look. Think about it. We would really love it if you came back to Bath."

"Like the Prodigal Son." I laugh.

"Yes, Dad. Just like the Return of the Prodigal Son."

Sixty

Mamma Mia

Dorchester, 2008

JULIE AND I ARE GETTING READY TO TRAVEL INTO London to see *Mamma Mia*.

"It's been ages since we've been to see a show," Julie says.

She is sitting at her little white dressing table, applying her lipstick carefully. I watch her blot her face with powder.

Earlier, I thought I was feeling excited about the trip. Perhaps it's not excitement. It could be anxiety. I am having difficulty distinguishing the two feelings in the pit of my stomach these days. Once the thought enters my head I feel the dark cloud descending. My mood is not good.

"It will be fun," I say, more to convince myself.

"Yep! Such bright and happy music. It can't fail to cheer you up." Julie has finished with her make-up and is putting up her hair.

Her comment annoys me further.

"What do you mean? Are you trying to say I am a misery-guts?"

"No, of course not, silly. I'm just saying it will be nice to go and listen to something happy. That's all."

I put my hand up against my ear. The ringing has come back with a vengeance. I hope that it will stop soon. It's no fun sitting in a noisy show with tinnitus.

We get on the train at Dorchester.

I sit looking out of the window. Julie is reading a book. She knows not to talk to me when I am in one of these moods.

We pull into Bournemouth station.

I can't breathe.

"Julie, I'm sorry," I gasp.

I stand up and grab my coat.

"I can't go to London. I can't go to the show."

"What?"

Julie is bewildered and picks up her handbag to follow me. Her paperback book lies forgotten on the seat.

I jump off the train and go and sit on a bench, my head in my hands.

My breathing is very odd, and the ringing in my ears is preventing me from hearing what Julie is saying.

She puts her hand on my shoulder. I can tell from her grip that she is furious, but she doesn't say anything.

"I'm sorry," I say again.

"It doesn't matter," Julie finally says through gritted teeth.

I know it matters a lot. This is the beginning of the end of the relationship.

When we get back home that night, Julie still hasn't spoken to me.

"It's impossible to explain," I say, in an effort to explain.

Julie has every right to be angry. It's happened a few times. I get ready to go out, to friends' houses, to the supermarket, even to church. I try so hard, but I just can't do it. Not being able to go to church is the one thing that really bothers me the most. I walk up the lane often and am so close. The ringing in my ears turns up to fever pitch and I have to stop and go back.

The fear is overwhelming. I have tried to describe it to Julie many times. The fear stops me participating in the world.

"Tell me something, Chris." Julie is speaking to me in a neutral tone. "Do you think if you had managed to stick it out, to make it to London. To go and see the show. That it might have been the start of your healing? You are denying yourself a way out of your grief."

Julie has a point. If I had managed to get my panic under control and make it to the show, it might have been the start of my healing process. My therapist has been saying it for a while.

"I'm just so afraid, Julie. I've never felt anything like this before. The fear is overwhelming. I feel so alone."

Julie glares at me.

"You're not alone, Chris. You have me. If you want."

She walks out the door and closes it gently behind her, leaving me. Alone.

Sixty-One

I Want to End It All

Dorchester, 2009

THIS IS IT.

I have come to the end. The depression has taken hold of me so deeply, I can't see a way out.

I sit down and pick up my fountain pen. I balance the heavy weight in my hand. I love this pen. Or I used to. My capacity to love anything has deserted me. Anne gave me this pen on our twenty-fifth wedding anniversary. I place the nib on the paper for too long. A blot appears. I rip off the top sheet of the pad and try again.

"Dear John," I start.

I am writing to Julie's brother. I have become quite close to him, over the past few years.

The words start to flow. Once I get into the rhythm it's not too bad.

I place the note in an envelope and seal it. I leave it on the bureau.

I catch the train down to the coast. There is a fishing shop there on the front. I stand and look carefully at all the paraphernalia. I think about how I will do it. Chains and a heavy weight. Would that work? Probably not. I turn and stare at the sea.

I walk down to the shore and close my eyes waiting. Waiting for someone or something to save me.

I put one shaky foot in the sea. Then, another. Soon I am up to my waist. I don't feel the cold, but the waves keep interrupting my thoughts with their insistent slaps. I start to cry. I miss Anne so much.

"What are you doing, Chris? You stupid man. This isn't you. This isn't the person I married. Think about Louisa. I left her in your care. Don't abandon her as well. This isn't the Chris I know."

I open my eyes; her voice is so clear.

"Anne?"

I look around wildly, to see if someone else has spoken. I know it can't be Anne. Anne is dead.

I am alone, apart from a dog walker throwing sticks for his Labrador further up the beach. I start to wade back to the shore. The shock of hearing Anne's voice causes me to break out in goosebumps.

I lie on the beach, staring up at the sky.

I am willing Anne to speak to me again.

Anne is silent. The silence feels approving.

I push myself up and walk back to the train station, feet cold and squelching in my shoes.

When I get home, Julie looks at my wet clothes and shoes.

"Oh, Chris. What have you done?" she asks, bringing her hand to her open mouth.

I cry so much I can't speak.

I get in touch with a local priest. I have reached crisis point.

"I know someone who works at Bath Abbey. She might be able to help," the priest says. "I am praying for you, Chris."

"I think you need to go home," says Shirley from Bath Abbey. I have called her late at night and am thankful she has answered.

"That's what my daughter Louisa keeps telling me," I answer sadly.

"So, why don't you go?"

"The decisions are too big. I feel completely lost. I have built this new life here in Dorchester with Julie, but nothing feels right."

"I will never tell you what to do, Chris. It's clear to me that you have reached crisis point. Some stability and direction might help you. I never want you to feel as desperate as you have today."

There is a long pause on the telephone.

"I think a frank conversation with Julie this evening might be in order."

I nod. It's not a conversation I want to have. I had made the decision to walk into the sea rather than to have that conversation. Julie is a good person. She doesn't deserve any of this, especially with all the heartbreak she has already been through.

My depression is so strong that I can't see a way out. I see now how wrong that is. I need to take back control of my life. It's what Anne would have wanted.

"How can you be so selfish?" Julie is sobbing.

"I know. I admit it. I'm selfish, disillusioned. I'm not a good person to have around. I think it's time I went back home. Back to Bath, back to Louisa. I'm causing too much damage and chaos here. I'm so sorry, Julie. You don't deserve this." I look at Julie, at the top of her head in her hands. I feel so much affection, regret, sadness when I look at her. I know I am doing the right thing.

Sixty-Two

Jekyll and Hyde

2003-10

I AM PERIPATETIC. I WANDER AIMLESSLY IN ALL WAYS. Personality, location, soul. I am lost.

I become a real loner. I have some routine, but not much. I go to the gym, I speak to Louisa, I spend money. This is now my life.

When I come back to Bath after my seven years in the wilderness, I am able to see more clearly. In Bath I get advice and help, and a normality is restored. I have come full circle.

Without the journey, though, I would not have been able to reach the correct mindset I have now, where I am able to fully love Pauline. I have found love in later life, against all odds. I think back to Anne again. That knowledge I gained when she died. That to understand yourself, to truly understand who you are, you have to be broken in order to rebuild. Her death (and therapy) helped me understand. I have to be able to look back in order to look forward again.

When I move to Dorchester and start my relationship with Julie, I react to life rather than grasp it. I am unrecognisable to myself. I think I know what I'm doing, that I am being kind to people, but in fact I am not. I am living a totally false life.

My new relationship with Julie is dysfunctional from the start; I just don't know it. She has just come out of a messy relationship herself and I am ashamed to admit that I feel pleased that I am not the only damaged person in the partnership.

It soon becomes clear that I behave less well than I think I do.

"You have no care for other people. You just care for yourself. You are selfish, Chris," Julie says, often.

"Well, Julie, bearing in mind what I've been through in my life... maybe it is my time to be selfish!" I retort.

"You can't just keep buying houses left, right and centre," Julie cries.

"Why not!"

I am unreasonable. I cannot see sense.

Our relationship lasts for five years. There are some happy times, and some less so. Throughout this whole time my depression deepens. If I were in my right mind, I would know I'm not being fair, that my heart isn't in it.

The lessons I learn from my relationship with Julie gives me a solid foundation for when I meet Pauline. I learn that grief can create a monster of you. That you can become abhorrent to yourself, and to others. That you only get so much understanding and 'good will' before people start to avoid you, if you start to misbehave.

Sixty-Three

Back Into the Arms of Bath Abbey

2010

I RETURN TO BATH.

Louisa takes care of me, and slowly things start to return to normal. I try and put Dorchester out of my mind as best I can.

I had a strong religious belief before, when Anne was alive. I had been so sorely tested with my faith when Anne died, I worry that I won't be able to reconnect to my religion in any meaningful sense again.

Louisa takes me to Bath Abbey the first Sunday I return to Bath. I am reluctant.

"Give it a go, Dad. You used to find so much comfort here. Your singing, your faith, the people."

"Ha. They abandoned me, remember? Your mum was so ill, but we got no support from the Abbey," I say, sadly.

"Did you ask for it?"

"Ask for what?"

"Support. Help. Apart from Simon, the priest. I know he came to visit you often."

Louisa is right, as always. Like her mother.

"Yes, he did. And no, I suppose we didn't ask. We became so involved with ourselves, managing the day to day, the disease."

"All I'm asking of you is to give the Abbey another chance," Louisa says.

"What are you afraid of?"

I am worried about returning to the Abbey. I'm afraid of many things.

"I'm afraid God won't forgive me," I say, quietly.

Louisa kneels before me.

"God always forgives. You know that."

I smile at her gratefully.

"I think I did. But I have forgotten."

When I come back to Bath and start my counselling, my therapist tells me the same thing. Go back to the Abbey. Maybe it's time.

I start with an evening service. I surrender myself to the wonderful music, the beautiful words. I have the opportunity to speak to the other members of the congregation. We start to feel like one big family.

I reacquaint myself with the Abbey community.

"How can I help?" I ask Susan, the formidable visitors officer one day. "I would like to become more involved in Abbey life."

"Well, we are currently looking for a steward, does that sound of interest?"

I think that sounds a marvellous thing to do.

I become a steward. I also become a guide. I particularly love this role, because of all the interesting people I meet. My depression starts to lift, and I find myself engaging with visitors who all have different stories to tell. War veterans who have lost limbs in war. Widows and widowers. People suffering, looking for solace. I could listen and talk to them for hours. Much like the work I was doing at Dorothy House, I find I have an aptitude for understanding all the suffering. After all, I had been there myself not so long ago. I start helping with the reading. I enjoy going into the scriptures in more depth, discussing the meanings. My faith is restored and getting stronger by the day.

I had lost my God completely through all the trauma of the previous few years. Little did I know that I had to go through that loss of faith to really find God again. Find him with such an open heart, such honesty that now I find myself in an enviable position.

I am not afraid of death anymore. I am not afraid of what happens, and I am now not afraid of the future.

The only fear I still feel is for my personal point of view. The memory of my deep depression and the unacceptable way I behaved whilst floundering in my seven years of wilderness are never far from my mind. I am not afraid of life on Earth.

My deep faith teaches me that there is another focus.

Sixty-Four

Working at Dorothy House

2011

AFTER I RETURN TO BATH FROM DORSET AFTER THE wilderness years, I am at a loss as to what to do, beyond re-engaging with my faith and with Bath Abbey.

I volunteer at Dorothy House, the hospice where Anne and I spent so much time during the later stages of her life.

I am asked a few times what compels me to want to return there, now my beloved Anne is gone. I am never quite sure how to answer, apart from my overwhelming need to give something back.

I never thought I would experience something as profound and awful as watching your wife die, so painfully slowly. I coped at the time because I become incredibly attached to other people. Particularly people who were physically present during the process, like Deidre, Louisa and the wonderful staff at the hospice where Anne and I spent so many happy days. You feel that they are the only ones who understand what you're going through.

I feel I want to talk about Dorothy House a little more. It is such an important part of my journey, and Anne's story.

Dorothy House was originally set up by a wonderful lady, Prue Dufour, in 1976. Her vision of providing care to patients with life-limiting illnesses was evident in all the time Anne was there. A woman of deep Christian faith, Prue wanted her patients to 'live well and die well'. Indeed, the name Dorothy means 'Gift of God' and it couldn't be more apt. Anne's quality of life was vastly improved by being offered respite there.

The grounds of Dorothy House are beautiful. The house itself is also lovely. A large, imposing house, made from Bath stone, with pillars on the porch, gables and large mullion windows that overlook the gently rolling lawn. I spent hours with Anne looking out over the neat stripes of the freshly mown grass, watching the lavender wave in the breeze. We didn't speak, just felt an intense peace. Those times form the happiest memories I have of her towards the end.

When we were at Dorothy House there seemed to be nothing to worry about. The peace was real. The outside world was firmly locked on the other side of the hospice door. There were nurses, doctors, physiotherapists, even our beloved chaplain to attend to everything. When Anne died and I didn't have a reason to visit, I found myself pining for the place.

Now I am one of the 1,200 volunteers who work there. I find great comfort in sitting with patients, listening to their stories. Sometimes they ask me about mine. I find it difficult to talk about Anne, but it is also liberating to discuss matters they understand more than most, living through it as they do.

There is an air of deep kindness at Dorothy House that can't help rubbing off on me. I appreciate this most at times when I don't feel kind myself.

I try and quell the rising resentment that this happened to me, to Anne. I feel anger often, which I try not to show. Sometimes it's too hard. Luckily, I have the support of the nurses who knew Anne before she passed away, and they are good at calming me down. I help them, but I don't know whether they fully understand how much they help me in return.

Only a few thousand people in the UK have Anne's condition, but at the hospice I encounter several patients with motor neurone disease, which is more common. All suffering looks similar, though, and I feel glad that I am able to give back as much as I can. When people die on my watch, it's so complicated. All the old feelings rush back, from when Anne passed. Somehow, it's thankfully so different, but it does bring back the sadness.

Sixty-Five

Joan

2011

I AM SITTING WITH JOAN, AN ELDERLY LADY WHO I VISIT weekly at Dorothy House. She has motor neurone disease.

"You can't understand what I'm going through," she says with a moan.

"You're right. I can't. Tell me how you're feeling. Is there anything I can do for you now?"

I am always careful not to try and talk about the past or the future too much. It feels important to care for Joan's immediate needs.

"No, I suppose not," she says, sighing and trying to get comfortable on her bed.

I pass her a glass of water and automatically swivel the straw, so she doesn't have to angle her head awkwardly. All the things I do for the other patients is muscle memory for me. I seem to know what they want before they do themselves. Anne always used to say that.

"Thank you. I feel a bit better."

Joan lies back with a little smile. It's a hot day, so I rise to open the window.

"So, tell me. Are you still grieving for your wife?" she asks. Her question is direct, but not unkind.

I sit back down beside her bed. "Well, of course I will always miss her," I say, carefully. "You might know already, but it's one of the conditions of Dorothy House. I am not allowed to volunteer if I'm in the raw stages of grieving too much."

"Well, how long has it been?" Joan is curious. "Since she died, I mean. How long has it taken you to get past the raw stages of grief, as you call it?"

I know she's asking because she's worried about Bert. She has talked before about this. She has anxieties about how her husband won't be able to cope when she goes.

Ha, I think. *I've heard that before!*

"Nine years since she died," I tell her, reassuringly.

I don't tell her that the grief doesn't go away. It just changes.

"Seven years," she says. Her mouth crinkles with the effort of speaking. Her hands smooth the small creases on the flowery duvet cover. I notice her hands need moisturising. I will do it before I leave. Anne used to hate it if her hands were dry and cracked.

"In seven years, Bert will still be in his sixties. He can get on with his life. Maybe travel, as you have. Even meet someone new." A single tear rolls down Joan's cheek.

I take her hand and lean forward.

"Bert will be fine, Joan. Look at me."

Joan turns her head slowly.

"If I can do it, so can he." I smile at her and pass her a tissue.

"Yes." She wipes her tear away and smiles back. "You are an inspiration, Chris, really. You are so kind and calm. You are a great comfort to me, and I look forward to your visits every week."

I am flattered. I often don't feel kind or calm, but I am pleased that she enjoys our visits. It's my only aim, to help others in the way that Anne and I were helped.

"You know, Joan, you have given me an idea," I say suddenly.

"What's that, Chris?"

"I am going to enrol on a bereavement course. Perhaps even study to become a bereavement counsellor. See if I can help people like Bert, properly. You know, to cope. When your time comes."

"What are you talking about, Chris! I am going to live forever." Joan flashes me an impish, lopsided grin.

We both laugh. We both know that's not true.

I take Joan's hand and rub in the moisturising cream I have taken from her side table. She closes her eyes in gratitude, and we sit in companionable silence for a while.

"You know, I think that's a marvellous idea, Chris. I love the idea of you helping Bert. When I can't."

Joan dies a month after this conversation.

I take the course, but I don't study to become a counsellor. I take on too much and life becomes overwhelming again. I take up singing again instead. A huge part of my previous life that is suddenly thrust centre stage in my life again. And thank goodness it does, or I wouldn't be in the position I am in now. Saved.

Sixty-Six

Perspective on Grief

2011

IT'S SUNDAY.

Louisa and I are walking along the canal, our favourite route. As usual I walk in silence. I am brooding about my recent behaviour.

"Louisa, what's wrong with me?"

"Nothing, Dad, why? Do you think there is?" Louisa is immediately concerned.

"Well, you seem to be doing well. You have a great relationship with Andrew. You appear to be getting on with your life. You haven't changed, really, at all. Of course I know you are sad, often, and the depression has been hard. You are still essentially the same Louisa, though. I don't feel like I'm the same dad you used to know."

We stop outside the pub we like to stop at for refreshments after our long walks.

Louisa looks at me, and I see uncertainty in her eyes. She is working out whether she wants to talk about this today.

"Oh, Dad, let's go in and have a good chat," Louisa suggests.

I follow her inside, and we set up in a cosy corner with a glass of red wine each. The fire is roaring in the corner and the smoke makes my eyes smart. I am already close to tears, so I am grateful to have an excuse if my eyes start to water. My uncontrollable crying happens frequently these days.

"Not a lot of people talk about the male aspect of grief," Louisa says.

"No, they don't," I say, sadly.

I have found this an isolating aspect of my journey. No one wants to talk to me about my grief. Even I don't want to talk about my grief.

"It must be hard for you. You are a man in his sixties, with a dad from a military background and a single-sex public school upbringing. It's going to be a completely different journey for you than for me," she continues. "I can cry when I want, and where I want. It's somehow acceptable. I doubt you feel the same freedom?"

"I don't," I admit.

I look at the swirling carpet on the floor. I feel strangely sleepy in this warm pub, with its fire and my lovely daughter. I want to stay here forever, not have to confront my everyday reality.

"You know I am in therapy, don't you?" I ask.

Louisa nods. "I'm pleased you were able to get help."

"I couldn't separate out what was grief and what was depression, you see," I explain.

"Has your therapy helped?"

"Who knows," I say glumly. "My head is a mess. I just feel so angry all the time."

The door opens and a draught of cold air comes in. We watch a group of four young lads walk up to the bar and order a round of drinks. They laugh, not a care in the world. I am envious of them.

"I think it must be hard for you. For any man," Louisa says, still looking at the young men. She swirls the red wine around her glass.

"I'm so glad you asked for help. That makes you braver than most. It can end badly. Especially if a man doesn't know that these are normal feelings and that they can be guided through it. Professionally, I mean."

I nod, thinking about Joan from Dorothy House and her husband, Bert. I wonder how he's doing. I should call him, really, see how he is. I have been scared to, as I don't want to take on his grief too. Mine feels overwhelming enough as it is.

Sixty-Seven

Assisi

2012

AFTER I RETURN TO BATH, I REALISE THAT I HAVE
missed out on a great part of my life. My spirituality. It was
a strange feeling, to understand that I had denied myself
the safety of talking to other like-minded people all this
time. Why had I tried to struggle on my own?

I go on a pilgrimage. To Assisi, to visit St Francis. I travel
with lots of people from Bath Abbey.

I step on to the plane. Every time I travel, I'm reminded
of the difficulties Anne and I used to experience travelling.
The hoists, the levers. It was all a lot to manage. Today I
travel with a light heart. I am not sure what to expect, but
I feel safe in the company of people who have worshipped
at the Abbey and elsewhere, parishioners, etc.

We walk part of the Via di San Francesco, through
stunning Umbrian countryside. I feel a sense of awe and

wonder at the feeling of enjoyment at the experience. Walking the Way of St Francis is hard on my aching knees, but my depression is lifting, and the sights and colours of the Italian scenery lightens my burdened heart.

We spend five days in the Casa del Terziario Franciscan Guest House. The nuns are fascinating to me. I take deep comfort in the monotony of the day. The rituals, the certainty of the schedule, the lack of choice allows my brain to rest. We visit the Basilica, bow our heads respectfully at the tomb of St Francis. We have meetings in the evenings where everyone opens up and shares their experiences.

"It's been hard for me," I admit to the others, one still evening. "I feel like I've been a bit of an outsider for so long. I feel blessed to be among you all."

The other pilgrims all agree. It's a very special atmosphere and experience we share. I hear stories of how people have suffered, how they had lost their partners, their sons, their parents. It's the first time that I am able to open up to other people who had suffered in a similar way to me. It is emotionally exhausting, but I find great comfort in hearing the other stories and how my fellow travellers had overcome and conquered their own grief.

St Francis was an amazing person. I learn all about his life, how he lived with the lepers over the years. I walk through the graveyard outside the leper colony, looking at the names of all the fallen soldiers from Commonwealth countries killed in World War Two.

On the last evening, after our supper, I break down completely. It is the turning point.

I am alone in my room, praying.

"You are back with Us," I hear.

I hear it as clearly as Anne's voice had been when I had walked into the sea that awful day.

This time I don't look around. I know who is speaking and I open my heart fully to the voice.

God has returned to my heart.

And I have returned to Bath as the Prodigal Son.

Sixty-Eight

Looking Back with Louisa

December 2018

LOUISA AND I WALK SLOWLY BACK FROM BATH TRAIN station. We have been on a rare trip together to London, to visit the Tate, somewhere Anne and I used to love going to together. We have been reminiscing about Anne, as we always do each December in the lead up to the anniversary of her death, and have decided to take a trip down memory lane by visiting a few places she really loved.

"You know, Louisa, I am eternally grateful you came into our lives," I say, squeezing her arm. "It wasn't an easy process, adopting you, but my goodness it was worth every probing question, social worker visit, all that."

"Thanks, Dad." Louisa laughs and slips her arm through mine. "I'm pleased I was worth all the effort. I never asked this when I was young, but now I have children of my own… well. It does sometimes cross my mind. You know, whether you regretted not being able to have a biological child of your own."

"Not once!" I exclaim. "Obviously it was difficult when we were trying for so many years, but the second I saw you, and held you in my arms… I knew. It was meant to be. And your mother felt the same."

Louisa smiles and says, "I have never doubted your love for me. It's just a natural question to ask, I suppose, if you are an adopted child. The fact you told me from the very start about the adoption meant I never worried about it."

"No, it was absolutely perfect. You are perfect. And the more I think about it, the more I am convinced it was God's plan all along." I give her a huge hug. We are approaching her house and Louisa stops to fish out her keys.

"Hey, I found something out the other day," I say, "about Friedreich's Ataxia. You might find this of interest. Do you know why the disease is so rare?"

Louisa shakes her head, distracted.

"Found them!" she says, triumphantly, jangling her keys.

"Well, I discovered that it occurs when both parents have the same disordered genes, and it's then passed on to their offspring!"

"Wow, no, I didn't know that. It hadn't even occurred to me that it was a hereditary disease," Louisa says. "Sounds like I was extremely lucky!"

We continue walking.

"As you know, your mother's parents grew up in Llanrhystud, a lovely Welsh seaside village. Their families had lived there for many years, going back generations. Elsie and Vernon, your grandparents, met at the village school when they were only ten years old. Of course they got married later, at the outbreak of World War Two. I'm thinking out loud here, but imagine. Just imagine… if there had been a case of first cousin-to-cousin coupling along the way in the family. Or worse! That would certainly explain the diseased gene, wouldn't it?"

Louisa gasps. "Poor Mum, I can't think of her as the product of some past incestuous indiscretion. Although you are right, it would explain it."

Louisa links her arm with mine and gives it a squeeze.

"I know it's hard to make sense of, sometimes," she says. "Her death. The way she died. The sheer injustice of it all. I often wonder why her? I always keep reminding myself it's just one of those things. Why not her? I suppose is the other side to the question. All I know now is that we have to keep talking about her. Keep her memory alive. It took so long for me to even be able to say her name out loud after she died. Now I see I was just prolonging my grief, by keeping it all in. I have found it much easier to cope now I'm able to tell stories about her. It keeps her with me, somehow."

"Yes," I agree. "We need to think of the happy times."

We arrive at Louisa's front door, and she turns to look at me.

"What do you miss most about her, Dad? I miss her cooking. Her love of animals. The way I would turn up at home, and she would have adopted another dog, or there would be an unfamiliar cat nestled on the sofa."

I smile, remembering too. "Those animals – she was so involved with them all day at the Dogs and Cats Home! She needed to be surrounded by animals. I think she would have brought them all back to live with us if she could."

"Her love of home cooking came from Grandma, didn't it? Remember those Welsh cakes Grandma used to whip up for our afternoon tea visits? Before she got ill?"

We both groaned in delight at the memory of those rich, fruit-laden scones.

"And that bara brith! Spread thick with that home-made butter she used to make out of double cream. Although I do think that's the reason your mum didn't use to bake so much. Elsie was a culinary expert, so she was always in the kitchen, popping this and that in the oven. No need for Mum to learn!"

"Yes, Grandma was an amazing Welsh woman, really. So accomplished, with her horticulture, career, cooking. We were blessed to have her in our lives. And Mum."

"What I loved was the pride they both had in their Welsh roots. I remember when I was much younger than I am now, when I first met your mum. I was playing a lot of rugby then. Got up to quite a good standard in my time." I smile modestly. "Well, our dates used to be quite funny sometimes. Mum loved rugby, thankfully. I was obviously pro-England and your mum was pro-Welsh. So your mum and I used to travel up to Twickenham to watch the internationals, and there was always this great battle. I was the only Englishman there in the group, cheering on my team. Your mum used to give back as good as she got, for her side."

I laugh at the memory. Louisa laughs too.

"I love hearing you talk about Mum in happier times, Dad. I really do. It brings back the good memories. I never used to think much about her being Welsh, because although Grandma had an accent, Mum didn't really, did she? Or have I forgotten?"

"No, she spoke very neutrally. I think it was all that time she spent in France, at Sorbonne. Her accent was sort of wiped out," I say in agreement.

We are both quiet for a minute, trying to conjure up the memory of her voice, before the illness so cruelly robbed it from her.

"Well, I'm so pleased I spent the day with you, Dad. It was a lovely way to remember Mum. We should do this a few times a year, you know. Go up to London or to old haunts. If we keep talking about her, and doing the things she loved... well, she's not really gone then, is she? She's still here, alive in our hearts."

Louisa raises up on her heels and kisses my cheek.

"Bye then, Dad. See you on Sunday. Come over with Pauline for lunch, the kids would love to see you both."

Sixty-Nine

Pauline and Anne's Different Approaches to Life Therapist Chat

2016–17

"I always say Pauline and Anne would have got on like a house on fire. It makes me sad that they never got to meet."

I am talking to Lucy, my therapist.

She nods her head. "You wouldn't have been open to a relationship with Pauline, if Anne was still here."

I laugh. "That's very true. What an odd thought. I can't imagine my life without Pauline. Anne was perfect for me then and Pauline is perfect for me now."

Lucy smiles. "This is progress, Chris. I am very pleased that you are able to see that there are positives in the past and also in the present. I think the therapy, and also this course you have been taking at Bath Abbey, has helped you enormously."

"It has," I agree. "I can see that bad things happen, and they are devastating and awful at the time and you don't know if you can get through. But out of those hardships you can really grow as a person."

"Absolutely correct. I'm so thrilled you have come to that realisation!"

Lucy sips her coffee and writes on her notepad.

I feel pleased, like I have passed some sort of test.

"Tell me about Anne. You mention her in our sessions often, about her illness and how hard it was for you at the time. But before she became ill, there must have been nearly thirty years of happy, or at least, more normal, times. Talk to me about her, let's see if we can shift your memories from the darker moments to something that you can look back on with a bit more light. I know it will be difficult for you, but let's give it a go."

I look at Lucy with trepidation. I don't really want to delve into my happier memories, the ones hidden deeper in my mind. That feels somehow more painful than thinking about the times when things were hard.

I take a deep breath. It's worth a shot.

"So. Anne was a very smart person, not a hair out of place. She had her sense of style from her mother, fastidious in her appearance, in her dress, clothes, everything. We used to laugh, as her wardrobe was overflowing with her purchases from those good clothes shops available to us at the time in Bath. You know, the classic tailoring of Aquascutum, Country Casuals. Even House of Fraser, a wonderful store in its time. There were so many independent and national retailers in Bath at the time. We rarely made trips up to London. If we did, we would only do so for a special occasion, and always catch a show or visit a gallery as part of the trip. They were magical times, really."

"That's interesting, Chris," Lucy says.

"How so?" I ask.

"In our previous sessions, you have talked about how you went on huge spending sprees after Anne died. Do you think you were trying to capture the essence of Anne and her love for the finer things in life? Trying to recreate the activities that had brought her joy, so that you could feel closer to her?" Lucy suggests gently.

I sit and think about it. That wasn't what was going through my mind at the time, but now I am not sure what my motivation had been. It's a possibility.

I shrug in response.

"Well, where we differed, I suppose, is that she was always independent. I needed her more. She always did her own hair, for example, for most of her life. Wouldn't go to a beauty specialist, anything like that. She was a very proud person in her outlook, and in every way, really," I say.

"Did that aspect of her personality spill over into other areas, then?"

"You mean her pride? Well, I suppose it did. She didn't open up very much to people because she thought it would have betrayed her dignity."

"Not even to you?" Lucy asks, leaning forward and looking interested.

"Well, a little more to me, but not much. Now I am in a relationship with Pauline, I can see what an open conversation looks, feels and sounds like. I suppose it's second time round for me. And for Pauline, of course, having been married before. So we have both learnt and grown as people. We can see the value of a good, honest discussion, and how it can save a marriage."

"So the value of being open and honest about your feelings – that is something that is different, something you have learnt. Are there any similarities you can pinpoint?"

I lean forward and rub my sore knee as I ponder.

"Now I think about it, the one thing that I have carried over from my relationship with Anne is the strict rule that we never, ever go to bed on a disagreement."

"That's a good rule."

"If we had an argument during the day, or whatever, like couples often do, we always, always made up. It meant that the next day was a fresh start, and the air was always clear. That is the rule I have with Pauline now, and it works very well for us, and has done so in the past."

"So you can see that having experiences that are both negative and positive can be learnt from, and you can grow as a person? Not having an open relationship with Anne has shown you the value of being more open with Pauline. Making sure that arguments don't fester has improved your chances of keeping the relationship more successful," Lucy states.

"Well, now you put it like that, I suppose so!"

"Any other similarities?"

"Many. Like Pauline, Anne was very much admired." I laugh fondly. "She had so many admirers. If we had parties at our house, our male friends used to be quite…

attentive, shall we say. My Princess Grace was the hostess with the mostess, and our home was always full. It used to sometimes make me feel quite jealous! But also very proud. We mixed with all the medical families and friends, particularly in our early marriage when her father was still alive. She was well known in Bath and really well liked."

"I suppose that's why it was such a shock when your friends fell by the wayside when she was diagnosed?"

I look down into my cup of tea. The milk has curdled slightly, and a few white specks float on light brown liquid underneath. I move it in my hands to disperse it whilst I think about this. I had been so hurt by all our more cultured friends dropping off, one by one, as Anne became more ill. I had wrongly assumed they would have been understanding, particularly in view of their profession.

"Yes, it was upsetting. Anne might have been physically compromised, and of course getting about was difficult. But her dry sense of humour never left her. Her love for all things cultural, music, that stayed the same. When she was still able to travel we used to go to the Bristol Vic quite a lot, Bath Theatre, that sort of thing. She loved Shakespeare, films like *Pride and Prejudice*. That's why I felt like I had hit the jackpot when I met Pauline. She is also very academic, like Anne was."

I smile as I think of Pauline. I still can't believe my luck.

"OK." Lucy glances at her watch. "I think we will leave it there, Chris, we can talk about this more at our next session. In the meantime, as homework, I would like you to look up Kubler-Ross when you get a minute. I think you might find it helpful."

Lucy stands up and takes my half-drunk tea from my hand. She looks at me kindly.

"I know this will have been hard for you, Chris, thinking about Anne in such detail. I do believe that the more you think about how your relationship worked with Anne – well, it will make you understand and value what you have with Pauline more."

Put like that, I cannot agree more.

I shake her hand and leave.

Seventy

Pauline

2016

THAT EVENING, I SIT QUIETLY ALONE IN THE LIVING ROOM. Pauline comes in with a glass of wine that I gratefully accept.

"How was your session today?" Pauline asks, sitting next to me. "You've been subdued since you got back."

I look at her and feel a huge surge of love.

"Sorry if I've been a bit quiet. I was talking about my relationship with Anne today."

"That's a huge step," says Pauline. "You've never really talked about that before, even with me. I don't know why, as we talk about everything else."

"Well, that's the point," I say. "This is what I realised today. I didn't ever really explore emotional depths with Anne. She was a wonderful woman in so many ways. But she wasn't a very open person. Her personality was proud and closed, and it was very difficult to scratch the surface. And even though I was a more emotional character…"

I stop, puzzled, as Pauline laughs.

"What?" I ask.

"Well, we certainly know that!" she says, squeezing my arm. "And I love you for it. Carry on."

"Well, Anne never gave anything away. And, as she was my first love, I never realised at the time that you could ask more, that you could delve deeper. So there we were, living very rich lives, doing all these things, having loads of experiences together… but I never thought to ask what she thought about anything! Isn't that odd? I only realise how odd that is now, after being with you, Pauline."

"How strange that you haven't always been like that, that this emotional openness is new! I think this calls for another glass of wine. Want one?" Pauline disappears into the kitchen and brings me back a refilled glass of red. She draws the curtains and stokes the fire before coming back to sit next to me. "Continue. Sounds like you made good progress with the therapist today."

"Yes. So, I think the reason I found it so very hard when Anne became ill, was that she had to suddenly lay bare all her life physically, and this was a massive thing for a proud woman like Anne. I think that vulnerability made her shut off even more from me emotionally. It's only now that I am starting to realise what that must have been like for me, from the distance of hindsight. I had to carry everything inside, no outlet, no way of talking about all the awful things that were happening to us daily as a couple."

"I am so glad you are able to open up to me, now," Pauline says, her usual kindness shining through as always.

"I don't want to sound like I'm diminishing my relationship with Anne. We had a good marriage. All I'm saying is that I am glad I have been able to grow from what I learnt. I can now articulate my feelings. I felt so much anger, which I could never talk about. I am sure that contributed to my behaviour during my wilderness years, as I call it. I am much happier and more balanced as a person now, being able to express my more extreme emotions of anger, or frustration. I feel that being able to open up helps me to survive."

"I'm really happy to hear that. I feel we have a very balanced relationship, lots of give and take. And I'm thankful for that. I'm off to bed, I have a very early start in the morning. Off to London for three days." Pauline gets up and gives me a kiss.

"I just want to say how grateful I am for you, darling," I call out. I can't stop myself. I feel that familiar gnaw of anxiety at the thought of her leaving me for so long.

"And I you, Chris. Goodnight, darling."

I watch her go.

I think about the fact that even though she is so much younger than me, her approach to emotions is somehow so much more mature that anything Anne and I experienced. It might be a generational thing. My generation was always much more stiff upper lip about everything. Not really as healthy. I think about the way I behaved in those years after Anne died, before I met Pauline, and my stomach sinks with that familiar feeling of regret and doom. I am so lucky to have learnt, grown and survived the wilderness.

Seventy-One

The Five Stages of Grief According to Kubler-Ross

2016

I scratch my head as I sit at my desk and pull over my notebook. I run my hands over the slightly raised pattern on the front and tap my beloved fountain pen lightly against my desk. I open up the notebook and raise my head to peer more closely at my computer screen.

'The stages of grief according to Kubler-Ross'.

I skim the words. Some jump out at me.

'Emotions go all over the place until we reach a place of acceptance'.

Ha! I laugh to myself at the mildness of the statement. *No kidding.*

I turn over to a clean page in my book.

I rapidly scribble five headings:

- » *DENIAL*
- » *ANGER*
- » *BARGAINING*
- » *DEPRESSION*
- » *ACCEPTANCE*

I stare at the words and think back.

Did my experience fit the pattern of these five, simplistic headings? I supposed they did, in a loose sense. Especially the 'DEPRESSION' heading. I certainly felt that emotion, viscerally.

I look at the screen again.

'Death is an unsolvable problem'.

I say the words out loud, slowly. Such a simple statement, but not one I had ever considered. It makes perfect sense now.

After Anne died, my mind tried to solve the problem of her inexplicable passing. I threw every trick in the book at it. I think about the methods I used to do that.

Spend more. Spend less. Do more. Do less. Love, but never too much.

If only I had read about these 'five stages' then. Would I have been more careful with myself? Kinder? More hopeful, perhaps?

It's no surprise my thinking was all jumbled. There was no solution.

DENIAL
I certainly tried to pretend Anne's death wasn't coming. It came as a huge shock, even though I had known for ten years it was going to happen. After it did, I tried to carry on as before: booking trips to visit Louisa, shopping, starting a relationship; behaving as if everything was normal, when it wasn't. I was completely numb during this time, floating through life.

ANGER
This was a new emotion for me, a normally jovial type of character. I was so angry all of the time, mainly with God. The anger was white hot and pushed all other emotions to the side. It caused me to behave badly, be careless with those left in the world that I still loved. It manifested itself in me physically: my body rebelled, I was in constant pain and caused constant pain to those around me.

BARGAINING
If I behaved a certain way, filled my world with possessions, experiences, people, then it would all be OK. But it was never OK. I was on a ride and I wanted to get off. But I couldn't. The only outcome from here, for me, was to sink into depression.

DEPRESSION
I tried everything to feel better and escape the crushing grief, really I did. Even to the point of trying to escape the world. Luckily I realised before it was too late. I really did have to go through the depression in order to bring

my grief to resolution. I suppose my numb period lasted throughout the wilderness years. I tried everything to stave off feeling anything. Predictably, nothing filled the void that Anne had left.

I carry on reading. Another line catches my attention:

'A crushing grief may well force you into a spiritual crisis'.

I write the word 'GOD' in big scrawling letters across the page.

GOD

This has been the one area of my life that I keep circling back to, that has bothered me the most.

I question myself now, as I have questioned myself constantly throughout the journey.

Do I… have I ever… had an appropriately strong faith? Why did I lose my faith?

How could he have let this happen to me? Was it all part of God's plan? How could he have allowed this to happen to my lovely Anne, who was as Christian in action as a person could be? She might not have been an active believer, true, but her kindness and willingness to help others was as close to the teachings of Jesus as any of the more vocal devout followers at the Abbey.

ACCEPTANCE

I trace my finger over the word 'ACCEPTANCE' several times.

It's the word in the list that resonates with me the most.

I battled to reach acceptance. I nearly died along the way. But I found it within me to accept my fate after I had moved back to Bath after my seven years in the wilderness.

Seven years is a long time. It's an excruciating length to stay trapped in grief, feeling anger, depression, denial. I'm only here because of a simple truth. After I reached rock bottom, I had people to help me see there was a future ahead. My daughter, my friends. And let's not forget my therapist, Lucy, who had a lot to do with showing me the light. She helped me so much. She made me see that in acceptance, I am able to find more love and realise I am enough.

How true that concept of acceptance is, I think. There is always more love. However you spread it or find it.

The fact that I am able to recognise the five stages I am looking at now, and how I went through them. I suppose that is also acceptance. My return to faith. My willingness to open my heart to Pauline. I have finally 'accepted' that my Anne is gone, I can think of her, grieve for her, and that there can still be a life afterwards.

A good life. A full life. A different life, but worth living.

I close my notebook. In it I have scribbled a few words, they will make sense to no one. Inside though, I feel lighter. Someone else's words have made my feelings more organised, tangible. I feel grateful to have found and read them.

Seventy-Two

Preston Church, Weymouth

October 2006

I HAVE STARTED GOING TO CHURCH AGAIN. TIM, THE rector of Preston Church, is a charismatic man, and we spend many hours talking about my life and what I had endured and am now going through. He becomes very interested in my story.

"Goodness, Chris, what a journey you have been on," he says. "I think the other members of the congregation might find what you have to say very useful. Would you consider giving a talk on about what you have been through over the past few years?"

"Oh no, I don't think I could," I answer, immediately. "Sad to say, my experience of the church is that depression is poorly understood. In all my time attending church I have never been offered counselling services."

Tim nods and says, "That is true. In our defence, we are clergy, not trained counsellors. We can give advice and help on matters of faith and spiritual health, but we do not have the skills to advise on the mind. This is why I think what you have to say on the matter could be useful. Have a think about it, anyway."

So I head home that night and think about it hard. Tim is right. Perhaps my story could help someone understand that depression is nothing to be ashamed of and there is help to be found.

"Tim?" I say, when he answers the phone. "I'll do it. I want to help people. If you think my story can do that, then I am happy to tell it."

"That's very selfless of you, Chris. I know this will be a hard subject for you to talk about. I… we… really appreciate it."

We discuss the logistics, and a time is set. I will give a talk on my journey to the congregation after the next Sunday evening service.

Seventy-Three

Talk on Depression
Preston, Near Weymouth

October 2006

"I would like to talk to you about life after Bath Abbey," I start hesitantly.

I stare at the expectant faces of the congregation. Many of the members have asked me about my background and my years of stewardship with Bath Abbey. There is an undeniable glamour attached to the place, and this magic has seemingly rubbed off on me somehow. People never tire of talking to me of the place.

I clear my throat.

"My faith in our Lord started at Sutton Valance school in Kent, where I was able to pursue my love of music, especially singing. I performed with choirs and choral societies for most of my life. This exposed me to the magnificent environment of Bath Abbey, where the wonderful music and singing became a major part of my spiritual life."

I stop and look at the audience. They are still with me. I plough on.

"My first contact with Bath Abbey was on the occasion of my marriage in 1965." I swallow as the memory of that happy day rises up.

"I knew on that day, Bath Abbey would always remain a special place for me. Later in the eighties, despite working with international companies such as Apple and Toshiba, with all the travel that entailed, I still found the time to become a sidesman, a visitor's guide, part of the lesson reader's team and I also assisted with the chalice. Eventually I found myself on the PCC and responsible for chairing various committees looking at the structure and working of the Abbey itself."

I know I am going into a lot of detail. I need to get to the point quickly, but I am struggling to find the words.

I raise my voice slightly. "My faith and devotion to God was growing stronger."

The members of the congregation murmur and smile at me. They see where I am headed. They want to hear of the strength of my religion, something they can identify with. They are in for a shock. This is not how the story continues.

I take a deep breath.

"In 1992, my wife with diagnosed with Cerebellar Ataxia. This is a very rare and life-threatening disability, affecting speech and the working functions of the legs and arms. There are only a few thousand people in this country suffering from Ataxia."

I pause. The audience look concerned, sad.

"Around the same time of her diagnosis, the Abbey was turning into a large organisation. It's the largest of the greater churches, with over 300,000 visitors a year, and the growth needed a reporting structure. In 2000, the Millennium Fund was launched to finance a massive restoration programme. It was a five-year programme, costing £6 million."

I look around – I am in danger of losing my audience. Their sympathetic faces when I mentioned Anne and her illness had turned to confusion. They don't understand why I am talking about a restoration project.

"I was offered the position of full-time Administrator. I agonised over the difficult decision to leave the exciting and fast-moving computer industry that had been part of my life for twenty years and so I turned to prayer. God answered and guided me to accept this big challenge. I felt I had been given a chance to help those who were still searching for their faith. Little did I know that my faith wasn't that secure, and I hadn't scratched the surface of what was to come."

I lean forward on my wooden chair and take a sip of water placed on the little table to the side. My mouth is dry from talking, and from nerves. I look up at all those expectant faces. I hope what I am going to say next isn't going to disappoint them.

"My wife died in December 2002. By this point I had to leave the spiritually rewarding position of Administrator to care for her deteriorating condition. My faith in God and prayers had helped me through one of the most terrible periods of my life."

There are sympathetic murmurs in the audience, and I catch the rector's eye from the back of the room. He gives me an encouraging nod. He's not going to like what comes next.

"I tried to believe that the experience of witnessing suffering and death would bring me closer to God. But. Suddenly I was alone and – as many of you have probably done in similar circumstances – asked the question, 'Why me, Lord? Why *me*?'"

I take a deep breath. "There was no answer I could find. The clarity God had always provided me wasn't there. I felt abandoned. I now know it was my grief, blinding me. But at the time, I felt he had deserted me at a time I needed him most of all."

I take another sip of water. I now cannot look at the audience. I can imagine their expressions.

"Bereavement follows many different patterns," I plough on. "All are painful, full of fear, anxiety, anger and suffering. Unfortunately I wasn't able to cope with life. Apart from my daughter, I shut everyone out. I became a recluse, full of remorse and anger. Unable to believe that God would play any part in my life again, least of all now. I left Bath and moved to Osmington. This escape, this attempt to lead a new life failed. It was not reality. I tried desperately to become involved in the new community. I found it impossible to connect with people properly or complete projects. The only thing that kept me going was physical exercise. It helped my mind and body and stopped me from having a complete breakdown."

I take another deep breath.

"There was no doubt. I was in a state of severe depression. I needed help. My life had no purpose or meaning and I was a misery to those who were trying to reach me and help me. I became suicidal, wandering the seashore, hoping a large wave would take me away."

I hear a gasp and murmur of, "No," from someone in the audience. I look up from my hands that have been clenched in my lap. I can't tell who said it. I see lots of bowed heads.

"This has a happy ending, fortunately for me," I say. "I was put in contact with a psychologist. Through a series of counselling sessions over a period of a year, he changed my life and I came out of darkness into the glorious light."

"How did you find your way back? To the light?" Stuart asks.

I like Stuart, he has always been open and affable whenever we have had occasion to chat. He has been the most welcoming to me. I am having to work a little harder to integrate with the others.

"Well, it was a long process," I say. "My bouts of depression became less. My psychologist introduced me to meditation. This daily exercise of mindfulness helped me to let God into my life again. I began to read the Bible and found comfort in the Gospels. I also began to realise the friends and family were praying for me. I had found my way back into God's world, and he had not deserted me as I had thought."

Stuart nods and smiles at me. "Thank you," he says.

"Well, it's good to be back and worship with fellow Christians again," I say. "I feel like I have a new 'family'

and a new life. Thank you for making me feel so welcome."
I smile and stand, signalling the end of my talk.

"Well done, Chris," Tim the rector says, afterwards. He shakes my hand warmly.

I am pleased that I had the strength and courage to talk so openly about what had happened to me, but I am nervous as to the response.

Seventy-Four

After the Talk on Depression

October 2006

After the talk, I wander over to the table with the tea and coffee pots. I pick up a fresh cup of coffee and take a biscuit. Just as I pop it in my mouth, I feel a tap on the back. I turn, hastily wiping away custard cream crumbs from my chin.

"Thank you so much for the talk, Chris." It is Sheila, one of the more active members of the church. I have always found her demeanour a little stern and aloof.

"Ah, I… hope it was OK. And that you got something out of it?"

"Yes." Sheila doesn't look convinced. "I am grateful that you felt brave enough to talk about your depression. It must have been a very hard time for you. It's unusual to hear a man talk in such an open way." Sheila takes a sip of her hot drink.

"It was, it was," I say, brushing more crumbs off my

sweater onto the floor. Sheila stares at the crumbs in a way that makes me feel uneasy.

"Don't worry, I will sweep up," I say, hastily, looking around for a broom.

Sheila looks up. Her large grey eyes are brimming with tears.

"It's just... I also find life difficult sometimes," she whispers.

I am slightly taken aback; I am not used to people opening up to me in this way; but, I reason with myself, it was the aim all along, so I am also pleased.

"Well, that was what I was hoping – to open up a topic to get people talking. I want to help people, particularly those who have been through a bereavement, or are lonely," I say gently.

"I am lonely. This is why the church, and this community, has been such a solace for me," Sheila says, wiping her eyes. "Silly me. But I am interested. What practical steps did you have to take to get better? I'm looking for the positives in life out there, but I am not finding it easy."

Stuart has now joined us. A few more people are milling about, and I can tell they are listening. I feel a burden of responsibility. What had worked for me, might not be the answer for anyone else.

"Well, I found it particularly hard," I say. "I had been through a double bereavement in a way." I pause, struggling to articulate this in a way that would make sense. "I had lost my mother in 1948, and a wife, who had taken the place of my mother in 2002."

"Taken the place of your mother? What do you mean?" Stuart asks.

"Well, my real mother had sent me and my brother away at the age of eleven from South Africa to be with my father in England. My mother had remarried someone who would not, or could not, tolerate us. My mother had no option then but to send us 6,000 miles away to a new country and to a father we had not seen for nine years."

"Nine years? Where on earth had he been all that time?" Sheila asks.

"He had been fighting the Japanese in Burma," I reply. "So my happy childhood, attending school in Cape Town, playing under the shadow of Table Mountain, having adventures on the family farm on Stellenbosch – well, that was destroyed on that fateful day."

"Very hard," Stuart agrees.

"So as you can imagine, I felt deserted and hurt. It had a destabilising effect on my life. That was, until I met Anne."

"You must have felt her loss deeply," Sheila says, sympathetically, placing her hand on my arm.

"Absolutely. Anne's death had rekindled the childhood memories of losing my mother. It was devastating."

"So how did you overcome this?" Sheila insists. She is clearly a woman who wants practical answers.

"Well, my turning point was during one counselling session after I had been through a particularly bad time. I had to turn inwards, look at myself from the perspective of view of myself, my future and my world. I had to delve deep into aspects of those points."

"Interesting. Here. Show us. Only if you feel comfortable doing that, of course."

Stuart hands me a whiteboard pen and points at the wall.

I start scribbling a list:

✓ VIEW OF SELF

    I'M VULNERABLE

    I CAN'T COPE

    I'M ALONE

    I'VE LOST SOMETHING PRECIOUS - GONE FOREVER

MY FUTURE

    IT'S ALL UNCERTAIN

    I WILL BE ALONE

MY WORLD

    IT'S DANGEROUS

    THREATENING AND FULL OF LOSS

I turn and look round. There are a few people peering at the board and nodding as if they understand the meanings behind the words.

"So, those are all quite dark thoughts you've written up there. How did you turn them around?" Sheila's interest is growing.

"Well," I say, "with the help of my therapist, I was able to flip my thoughts. Like this."

I turn back to the whiteboard and start writing again.

VIEW OF SELF

    I'M NOT SO VULNERABLE

    ACTUALLY I AM VERY RESOURCEFUL

    I HAVE GAINED SOMETHING PRECIOUS AS WELL AS HAVING LOST (LIKE ALL OF US HAVE AT TIMES)

    I'M NOT ALONE - IN FACT I'M QUITE CONNECTED

MY FUTURE

    ACTUALLY SOME THINGS ARE FAIRLY PREDICTABLE AND THOSE THINGS UNKNOWN WILL BECOME KNOWN

    I WILL BE CONNECTED

MY WORLD

    IT CAN ALSO BE EXCITING, SAFE, REASSURING

    LOSS IS ALSO BALANCED BY GAIN

Sheila comes up and gives me a hug. "Thank you," she says. "This is something I can go home and do right now. I am so pleased you were open enough to give your talk. Very brave." She squeezes my arm again and picks up her coat to head out into the night.

Stuart also comes up. "Bravo, old chap," he says. "Not a lot of fellows would have had the nerve to stand up and do what you did. I certainly found it useful. Not a lot of support available for people like us who have depression." Stuart gives me a wink. "I feel I know you a lot better now. Welcome to the community." Stuart shakes my hand again and follows Sheila.

I head home buoyed by the evening. It is so important to talk, I realise it more and more. Tim congratulates me again and several other members of the congregation came up afterwards to share their stories. It seems that everyone has a hardship to overcome. I am happy that my story was a catalyst to them feeling less alone.

Seventy-Five

Meeting Pauline
The Three-Minute Rule

November 2014

I FIRST LAY EYES ON HER IN THE SOUTH TRANSEPT OF Bath Abbey. She is dressed in the colours of a radiant sunrise, standing off to the side, alone, clutching a cup of coffee.

"Hello," I say, approaching with my hand outstretched. "I'm Chris."

"Hi, I'm Pauline," she says, offering a wide smile and shaking my hand.

"I'm not sure I've seen you at the Abbey before?" I say. "And I should know, because I'm here most weeks."

"Oh, dear, you've caught me out there. Yes, this is my first time."

"In that case, welcome. Are you just visiting Bath or…" I moderate my voice so as not to sound too enthusiastic, "…new to the area?"

"I'm new to the area." She pauses. "Forgive me if I'm speaking out of turn here…" she says, a twinkle in her eyes, "…but do you really want to know? Or are you just following a two-minute meet and greet rule?"

I laugh, surprised. She is a bright one, no doubt. We have been speaking for less than two minutes and she has already got the upper hand.

"OK, so that's me caught out. Yes, we do have a three-minute rule here. But please, rest assured I am always genuinely interested in the conversations I have," I say, suddenly desperate to make sure she knows my motives are genuine. I pause while she takes a sip of black coffee. "You know about the three-minute rule, do you?"

She shrugs. "Kind of. I was just testing the water."

"It certainly helps break the ice," I say. "We like all our visitors to feel welcome."

As longtime steward and guide at the Abbey, I feel personally invested in Bath Abbey.

"So, what do you do?" I ask. "Don't tell me, something that involves detective work?"

She laughs at my joke. "Oh no, nothing as fabulous as that. I'm a lawyer."

"Oh," I say. "I should have guessed."

I am impressed and intimidated in equal measure.

"So, both beautiful *and* bright!" I say clumsily. I can feel myself blushing. Was I being too forward? It had been so long since I have found myself even remotely attracted to anyone, maybe I'm way off the mark?

"I'm not sure I'm either, but I like a compliment so, thank you." Pauline tilts her head graciously. I admire the long lines of her neck and we stand in silence for a few moments, sipping our hot drinks.

"So, where have you come from?" I say, trying to extend the conversation.

"I have lived all over, but most recently, Warminster."

"Ah, how lovely," I say, racking my brains for any conversational snippet I might have on that part of the world. *A military place. Could she be connected to the army? A soldier's wife, there's a thought.* I glance down at the fourth finger on her left hand. Nothing. Not even the tell-tale indent of someone who has worn a ring and removed it after years. Pauline spots me looking at her hand and gives me a wry smile.

"What made you move here?" I add hastily. Caught out again. I feel like a teenage boy.

Pauline doesn't instantly reply. Instead, she looks around and makes a wide gesture with her arm.

"Bath is wonderful for so many reasons, I'm sure I don't need to tell you. I love the cultural side. There is so much more going on here than in Warminster, that's for sure. In Bath you get the concerts, the theatre, the restaurants. The breadth and scope of things to go out and do in this city is wonderful. I would even go as far as to say I prefer it to London. Do you enjoy music?"

I feel on more comfortable territory now.

"Ah, absolutely, I have sung many times here at the Abbey at various concerts. Singing is my not-so-secret passion," I admit.

Pauline's eyes light up.

"That's great! I also love music, although I only listen

to it. No one in their right mind would want me in their choir."

"I'm sure you're not that bad!" I laugh.

Having struggled to get into the flow and a little tongue-tied at first, I now feel as if I've known her for ages. I felt a familiar stab of guilt and fleetingly think of Anne. What would she make of Pauline? Here I am. Practically flirting.

"Well, Chris. Our three minutes must surely be up by now. Maybe we could go to a concert together and continue this conversation. Preferably without a time limit?"

I catch my breath. Was she joking or did she just ask me out on a date? I am so out of practice with all this, I can't tell.

"Yes, yes. I would absolutely love that."

"Great. Let's do that sometime then." Pauline delves into her handbag and passes me a card. I look at the thick cream calling card and slip it into my jacket inner pocket.

"Right, I must dash," Pauline says, placing her cup and saucer on the table next to the coffee machine.

Alarm bells started ringing in my head. *She must be married, after all. Or have a partner. Perhaps long-divorced or a widower? Hang on. How old is she?* I look her up and down surreptitiously. She is at least twenty years younger than I am, I estimate. My heart sinks.

I've got it wrong. There is no mutual flirtation; she is just being friendly. This young, confident lawyer wouldn't be interested in me. What an old fool I am, to think anything different.

Pauline shakes my hand again and holds it for a second longer than I'm used to.

"It was so good to meet you, Chris. Call me, won't you?" She releases my hand and runs her fingers through her dark, cropped hair, flashing me another smile. I watch as she exits the Abbey.

What has just happened? This beautiful creature in dazzling red has just turned my world upside down. I know I won't be able to take my mind off her for some time to come. I take the card out of my pocket and look at it again. The guilt about Anne starts to rise up again, and I make a snap decision.

As exciting as I had just found our brief interaction, I already know I won't call Pauline. The risk of having my heart broken at this fragile state in my life would be more than I could bear. I have only just managed to find myself on an even keel after Julie and my seven years in the wilderness.

No, I think. *Pauline is far too risky a friendship to strike up at this stage.*

I turn to join a small group of regulars, all seemingly so drab now in comparison, and try to concentrate on their chatter. Anything to distract me from thinking about Pauline and her vibrant face.

I think this is what it means to experience the mythical 'love at first sight'. How lucky I am to have experienced it twice.

Seventy-Six

Falling in Love is One Thing

Present Day

I NEVER EXPECTED TO LOVE AGAIN. I CERTAINLY never predicted finding a love that would be so pure and exciting. My years in the wilderness had seen me try and fail to find a love like this, and here I was, falling into it by accident.

Love in later life isn't easy. It brings with it so much complexity yet so much joy. Life never pans out as expected. When you start a relationship in your youth, there is no residual 'baggage' as a result of falling in love. No tricky past, full of characters you have loved and lost to weigh you down. No troublesome present complete with new challenges.

It is quite easy to be totally carefree during young love, I think, looking up from my morning crossword to stare out of the window as I mull over this idea.

As a young couple, you can set off on a magical journey together, naturally and romantically. You can gallivant along happily, doing all the things young couples in love do, and not give it a second thought.

Things are rarely complicated in youth. During the first flush of love other people tend to be excited for you and cheer you on your way. They become just as caught up in the romance of the engagement and the excitement of the wedding as you are. Your first home together, your first pet, your first baby, perhaps. You can lay down the foundations of your future life with optimism and hope.

It's not the same at all with love in later life, I conclude, going back to my crossword.

But no less rewarding or wonderful for it.

Pauline and I had been talking about this very subject an hour ago, over breakfast, just before she had set off for London. It had been a light-hearted chat. One of those conversations that should have brought us closer, especially as we were talking about a topic dear to both our hearts. Each other.

"Does it ever bother you that I'm older? That I've lived a whole life before I met you?" I ask.

Pauline looks surprised. "You know this has never been something that has worried me!"

I laugh in relief. "It must mean I'm wiser... if nothing else. As someone who has already navigated his way through a marriage, I am clearly a better bet than a younger man who has had no previous experience in the area. Much more likely to be trustworthy, financially stable, and generally a more acceptable and rounded individual, wouldn't you agree?" I tap my hand on the table for emphasis, causing Pauline to smile.

"Right, I must go and finish getting ready, or I will never catch that damn train." Pauline stands up and brushes the crumbs off the front of her dressing gown before disappearing upstairs.

When she comes down again, she is transformed. Before me stands the quintessentially competent lawyer, resplendent in her standard work attire of grey skirt suit and silk blouse, plain silver jewellery applied, dark hair brushed and glossy. I always get a thrill seeing her dressed up like that. I am so proud of my wife. I am even proud of the job she does, even if that job takes her away from me so often.

Pauline kisses me and dashes out of the front door with her overnight bag, promising to be back tomorrow evening in good time.

"Perhaps we could catch dinner in town?" she calls back to me, waving goodbye. I watch her go with the usual lump in my throat.

I hate saying goodbye. It never seems to get any easier.

I sit now at the breakfast table, swirling the remainder of my coffee in my cup, thinking back to our conversation. Pauline is a precious lady, with a generous soul and kind, open heart. I thank God daily that I was able to have shaken off the wilderness years. If I had let my depression destroy me, I would never be sitting here, content, in love and fully enjoying life. It is World Mental Health Day today. The subject is all over the press, all over social media. Everyone sharing their stories. So many, many stories.

The irony is not lost on me. Thank goodness the conversation is easier now. The awareness is out, the stigma slowly falling away. So many people's lives, helped and saved. I make my way over to my desk and open my notebook. I keep a gratitude journal, and the first line is always the same:

1. I AM GRATEFUL FOR LOVE. PAULINE IS MY LOVE.

Seventy-Seven

Bath Abbey
Second Meeting

12th December 2013

MY LEG IS CAUSING ME SOME TROUBLE, A CONSTANT painful reminder of my previous sporting days. Having been such an athlete, I am frustrated by my physical limitations. I find it difficult to stand unsupported through a concert these days, requiring a high stool as back up in case my knees give way.

We are singing one of my favourites, Verdi's *Requiem*, but in truth I can't wait for it to be over so I can take a bit of a rest. I fear my days singing these long pieces standing up might be numbered. I feel a pang of sadness. A short moment of silence follows the final electrifying 'Libera Me' of the soaring soprano and the deep, rich tones of my fellow tenor and basses. I can't help but smile at the enthusiastic applause that quickly follows.

Someone in the audience catches my eye. It can't be. But there she is.

Pauline.

It has been a few weeks since I first met Pauline in Bath Abbey, and I didn't expect to see her again. But here she is, watching me perform. I hope that I haven't been wincing from the pain in my knee. I now want to appear as vital as I have ever been. She sees me looking at her, and I nod at her slightly. She smiles back and returns the nod. My heart soars. Then she picks up her handbag and leaves quickly, heading out the back of the hall. The other audience members are still clapping. My heart sinks.

Why didn't she wait?

Pauline has been occupying my mind more than I deem sensible these last few weeks. It feels like madness. We had only exchanged a few words. Why on earth should I be thinking about her? As I noticed at the time, she is clearly a fair few years younger than I am. There is no reason to believe she would give me a second thought after our little chat. And yet. There was something in that nod that I can't quite shake. A warmth, and a flicker of something else. Could it be interest? I can only hope.

A few days later, on a Sunday just before Christmas, I make my usual way to Bath Abbey, taking in the beauty of the city on a quiet morning. Pauline is sitting there, right in the front pew, head bowed in quiet contemplation. Slipping into a seat a few rows back, I can hardly believe it. I struggle to concentrate during the service. I make a beeline for her at the coffee morning afterwards.

"Good morning! It's Pauline, isn't it!"

"Oh… hello…" Pauline looks a little surprised, as if she wasn't expecting to see me there.

It knocks my confidence a little, and I continue with caution.

"Was it you I saw at the concert the other night?" I ask, now uncertain. Maybe it hadn't been her after all, and I had been nodding at a total stranger.

"Concert? What concert?" Pauline answers, neutrally.

I can't help but stutter. "I'm so sorry, I was sure I spotted you in the audience at a concert I was singing at. I must have been mistaken, please forgive me."

Pauline gives a short laugh.

"Sorry, I was just pulling your leg. Of course I saw you. Great concert. You were resplendent in red," she replies, with a mischievous grin.

I feel my anxiety easing. Could it be she was now flirting with me? Maybe, just a little.

"I enjoyed that concert very much. In fact, there's another one coming up fairly soon. Perhaps we could go together?" Pauline asks the question in a very matter-of-fact way, as if she is commenting on the weather.

I, on the other hand, can hardly contain my eagerness.

"That would be really wonderful, I would like that very much. Here, take my email, you can get in touch and let me know when and where!" I produce a pen from the inside pocket of my jacket and scribble my details down on a napkin. It is less elegant than the cream business card Pauline hands me the first time we met, but it will have to do. She takes the napkin and tucks it into her smart leather bag.

"Great," Pauline says, with a smile. "I will be in touch. Now, I know you must get off and mingle. I am sure the required three minutes have long passed, and yet here you are, still chatting to me. The congregation will begin to suspect favouritism."

On that parting note, she drains her coffee cup and leaves.

This must be fate, I think. Meeting twice and sharing such warm conversations both times cannot be ignored.

I will make sure to telephone her this time.

"Pauline?" I feel nervous; my tongue is dry in my mouth. I stare at the cream business card. I'm certainly not going to forget her name, that's for sure. Pauline ———, Senior Partner.

"Yes?"

"It's Chris. Um. There is a Christmas concert, next week Friday. I'm sure you are busy, and your schedule means you most probably can't make it, but just in case you can… would you like to come with me?" I hold my breath.

"I would be delighted. Just tell me where."

I can barely breathe. We speak for several minutes about the concert and other forthcoming events, both at the Abbey and other venues in Bath. I find her just as easy to chat to over the telephone as I did at the morning service.

When I put the receiver down, I can't help it. I punch the air as if I have just won a rugby tournament.

I am going on a date with Pauline.

Seventy-Eight

Holding on to Love

Bath, Present Day

I DO SOMETIMES WONDER. IF I HADN'T HAD THE experience of my first marriage, would I have grasped the opportunity of loving my wonderful Pauline so deeply and so readily at this stage of life?

I might have put obstacles in the way:

"She works in London..."

"She is too young..."

"We might not be interested in the same things..."

These are the sort of comments that sometimes flit briefly through my mind. The 'wilderness years Chris' would have listened to those doubts. Maybe.

But deep down, I know the answer would always be yes. There is no denying it. I had been smitten with Pauline from the moment I laid eyes on her. Once I started getting to know her better, there was no chance of it going any other way. I fell hopelessly in love, and would be until the end of time probably, regardless of whatever else goes on around us.

"Do you think our situation is unique?" I ask, passing her the sandwich I had prepared earlier that morning. We are on a train up to London. We are going to the theatre that night, and I am excited to be with my new wife.

"What situation?" Pauline asks, scribbling in her notebook and taking an absent-minded bite of her egg and cress.

"Well, this. Us. Finding such strong love in second marriage. In later life."

Pauline looks at me. I can tell her mind is still whirring over the complex problem she is trying to tackle for work.

"Sure," she says, absent-minded. "I think there are loads of us around. Particularly now internet dating is so easy. There just isn't the stigma about going online and finding a partner. We were lucky, we met 'in real life', as they say, these days, but I have lots of friends who are meeting like-minded men in their forties, fifties and sixties. It's very common now."

"I guess so. I am just curious as to whether their relationships work as well as ours. Every person will undoubtedly turn up to a partnership with a real bag of problems, issues and complex family situations. Falling in love when you are young doesn't really come with all that," I say.

"I suppose problems are highlighted, and possibly get more serious as you get older. But love is love, and can be just as delightful and wonderful in later life as in the first flush of youth. People just need to work a little harder, is all.

Bitterness, sadness, all those burdens of past relationships. Well, they just have to be put to one side."

"Yes," I say slowly. "But sometimes it's not that easy, is it? I just wish I could go out onto the streets of Bath, or London, right now, and give all the young lovers laughing and cuddling their way towards their first marriage some advice—"

"And what advice would that be, oh great relationship guru?" Pauline says, with a fond smile.

"'Appreciate this!' I would say to them," I say, pausing for dramatic effect. "'Life will never be this uncomplicated again.'"

Pauline puts her pen down and cranes her head towards me.

"Are you saying I'm complicated, Chris?"

"No," I say hastily.

Pauline laughs. "I'm pulling your leg. I know what you mean. Life just gets more and more tricky along the way. I get that. But I think it can enhance a relationship. If the foundation is strong enough."

"True," I agree. "Like us."

"You OK, Chris? You are asking a lot of deep and meaningful questions for…" Pauline peers at her elegant dress watch, "11am on a Friday morning…" she says, affectionately.

"Yes, yes," I say. I smile back at her and pick up my sandwich. "I am just feeling very grateful to have found you. There was a time when a simple train ride like this could have set off a panic attack. I'm just thinking about how far I've come. And a lot has been to do with finding you." I pick up her hand and kiss it. "Thank you."

"Ha." Pauline laughs and picks up her pen again. "It's my pleasure."

I watch her working, my heart filling to burst with deep affection.

For the rest of the journey I continue to mull over young love, slightly nostalgically.

When young love ends – either through separation, divorce or death – you have two choices, I think. You can give up or rebuild another life.

I had somehow done both. Until recently, I had found myself on a self-destructive path that had nearly been the ruin of me. This new love has come about by sheer accident. Pauline has been my saviour in every way. And I am surprised to find that all I had been through with Anne had surprisingly given me the tools and strength of character to tackle everything that comes part and parcel with a second marriage. I am now a better person, and a better husband. I am glad I stuck around to discover this.

Seventy-Nine

Mother and Saying Goodbye

Present Day

THERE IS A MEMORY THAT WILL STAY WITH ME TO THE end, I think.

I can still remember the last goodbye, at Cape Town dock, in 1948. One of the most affecting moments of my life.

I can still see the image of my mother waving at me cheerfully, as I sobbed at the sight of her getting smaller and smaller on shore. I was already feeling seasick on board that ship, setting out to sail across the violent seas towards England towards my aloof father and a strange new life.

The worst goodbye. I knew what it was. An abandonment.

To get someone like Pauline to understand the depth of my anxiety around saying goodbye is quite difficult. Anne had understood, but only from an abstract perspective. She had less cause to leave me on a daily basis than Pauline. When Anne did leave me, it had been brutal and final, but at least she knew nothing of how it affected me. So that was something.

Pauline is getting close to appreciating the extent of my trauma. My work with a therapist has helped enormously, but I still find it hard to get the depth of emotion across. Every time Pauline leaves to go to London for work, I feel a deep feeling of anxiety deep in the pit of my stomach. She goes for three or four days at a time, and I am left here. What if she doesn't come back? I am aware that this sort of behaviour doesn't help my cause, as there is nothing really that Pauline can do. She loves her work and gains a lot from it. It doesn't stop me pleading with her almost daily to stay at home and work, rather than make the long train journey into Paddington. Pauline is wonderful, and normally laughs off my fears and kisses my forehead goodbye, promising to be back before I know it.

I think back to when we were courting, before the marriage. A time when it was all carefree and wonderful, our diaries full of dinner dates and dances. It had been an exciting time. We attended so many wonderful concerts, restaurants and shows. We still do. All the things we love to do together.

I take a moment to marvel at my good fortune in meeting her.

Both of us in desperate need of love; both hurt and disillusioned in our own way. And yet, we were both open to the possibility of finding each other under the beautiful arches of Bath Abbey.

We had been successful in leaving the past behind us.

"We have been brought together to save each other," we often marvel together. "So compatible, we can confront the dark days together."

What is the most important thing in a relationship in the end? Is it the love? Is it overcoming difficulties? Or is it the realisation that it is all of the above, and really, you must just snatch the moments of joy and run with them?

Eighty

Exploring Christianity

Present Day

I PAUSE. ONE OF THE NOTICE HEADINGS IN THE Abbey's weekly notice sheet catches my eye.

'Exploring Christianity – Prayer and Spirituality'.

I am instantly intrigued. I read on.

"*Would you like to broaden your understanding and practice of Christian prayer and spirituality? This is a ten-week programme supported by the Diocese of Bath and Wells.*"

I would, I think to myself. I can see, as it says, that it would be a wonderful way to enrich my faith.

I speak to Pauline about it when she returns from London that night.

"Something caught my attention this morning," I say, thoughtfully.

"Oh, yes, what was that?" Pauline asks, unpacking her

briefcase and setting all her papers out on the pale oak of the dining table.

I sigh. We will be eating at the kitchen counter, or our laps tonight.

"Well, I saw it in the Abbey notices. It's a ten-week course on Christianity."

I wait.

"Oh, yes?" Pauline sounds quite interested; her head is deep in her briefcase, rustling around for her pen.

"I am considering it, but it might be heavy-going, and full of academics, theologians. Even people training to be priests, I imagine."

"Are you? Training to become a priest?" Pauline laughs, finding her Mont Blanc and holding it aloft in triumph.

"No, of course not. You're right. I won't think anything more of it."

Week after week, the same notice appears. I cannot let it rest. My mind whirrs with the excitement of possibility.

I am not an academic. There would be lots of coursework and I'd have to commit to meetings every Monday afternoon for ten weeks. Then other modules would follow. It would take up a big chunk of my time. I think about all the reasons as to why I can't commit to the course.

One evening, I find myself alone again. Pauline is up in London. My mind cannot rest. I think about the course.

I remember being asked to join another foundation course by Bath and Wells some twenty years ago. I had turned it down at the time. I suddenly realise that I had been one of the 'floaters'. The reason I had turned it down was because I didn't know at the time what real faith was.

I pray. I ask God to help me reach a decision. The answer comes back loud and clear.

I contact the facilitator.

"That's great news, Chris. I think you will find it very enriching and rewarding," she says. "It's a two-year commitment, but I'm sure you will rise to the challenge."

I gulp. What I had thought would be a ten-week course has suddenly expanded to two years.

I still commit. "Sign me up," I say, impulsively.

I tell Pauline. She is thrilled.

"At least I know you will be kept busy and out of mischief whilst I am away with work during the week," she says, her lovely eyes dancing.

I start the course the next week. I am excited to travel with St Paul on the 10,282 miles he travelled on his three missionary journeys. Through the readings, I walk beside Jesus and St Paul every day. I love the lively group discussions, and the friendships and trust that have developed between us.

Many of the topics about 'love' are human stories that relate to our everyday lives. We share our own stories of grief, divorce, marriage. We talk about how we came to faith.

The course gives me new vision and understanding about things I have glossed over in my life.

Eighty-One

The Task
The Prodigal Son Parable

Present Day

HALFWAY THROUGH THE COURSE I FIND MYSELF opening up in a way I never thought possible.

Throughout the last few years, I have often referred to myself as the Prodigal Son.

Let me explain why.

After I regain my faith after my years in the wilderness, I find that Luke 15: 11–32, the Parable of the Prodigal Son, jumps out at me as the pearl or the crown of all Jesus's parables.

I find the need to be reassured that I am worshipping a forgiving God. I read the passage over and over, as I have many times over the years, particularly during my dark times. I reread it for the hundredth time in preparation for my course assessment this week.

For some reason my mind wanders and I put myself in the place of Jonah. I imagine myself small, helpless, facing the yawning mouth of a huge whale, where everything will be dark. I know what it's like to be swallowed up by a big fish and to cry out.

"Lord, give me another chance!"

The Christianity course brings me a lot of joy. It also brings up the hurt and also some understanding of my past.

This week, the theme is grace and forgiveness. I take the passage of the Prodigal Son to read and discuss at the meeting.

The parable is in response to the grumbling Pharisees and Scribes. It's a complicated theme – I churn the ideas around my head. Is the famine representative of the Prodigal Son's behaviour? Do we want to see people punished before we forgive them?

"This is one of my favourite passages," I say. "There is just so much in it from the perspective of the father and his sons. The younger son asking for his inheritance is a terrible thing to do in any society, but particularly in the Jewish culture. It's like saying, 'My father is now dead to me.'"

"Interesting. It is also terrible in Jewish culture to look after pigs, which the son has left the family home to do," the course leader, Angie, agrees.

"Exactly. So his father is like God, who will always forgive and rejoice, with the sinner who is coming back to faith. Most people would be angry in the elder son's position. It is very hard to understand the justice behind the idea that if someone repents, they are immediately forgiven, regardless of sin."

"So what does that mean for the real world?" asks Janine, one of my course colleagues.

"I think that it means we have all made mistakes and done things that have taken us away from God, the Father. We all need forgiveness. I think the most important message of the parable is that we get far more from God than we deserve, but that God is always there for us," I say, pensively.

The other course members nod in agreement.

"But how would we interpret this if we were non-believers?" Angie asks.

"I think you've got to let your children go, and make their own mistakes," I say, slowly. "Of course we are always there for them, and support them, whatever they do. The son felt the need to go off and see the world, escape his parents. It was hurtful to them, and a great betrayal, but they were still there for him on his return. It's like life today. Lots of people are struggling to survive. This parable is useful, as it sends out an overwhelming message of love and support. I can see the father in the story offering forgiveness to his son."

"And how do you see this echoing in your own life?" asks Angie.

"Well…" I pause.

This is the hardest part to put into words. I am reminded of the talk I gave to members of Preston church, all those years ago. I look around quickly.

It had been a similar room, the one in which I gave my last talk. The pale yellow walls, the dark, mismatched chairs. The over-bright lights illuminating the synthetic patchy carpet. I had been heartened then by the people who had come up to me afterwards to tell me how my words had touched them, how they were struggling themselves.

I wonder what the response will be today.

"When my first wife was diagnosed with Friedreich's Ataxia, a form of motor neurone disease, it was a terrible shock."

Janine tuts sympathetically. "I can imagine," she says, quietly.

I continue, "She died ten years later, a lingering, painful and cruel death. I watched all her bodily function collapse. Our house became a nursing home. I am ashamed now to say that I was angry with God. He had taken away my loving wife after thirty-eight years of happy marriage."

I swallow back unexpected tears.

Janine leans forward in her chair, rubs my arm, and says, "I'm so sorry to hear that."

I continue to blink, trying not to sob openly. The hurt is still so vivid after all these years.

"You say you were angry with God, and yet here you are on this course. How did you come round to faith again?" Angie asks, gently.

"Well. It was a long road and it wasn't easy. I was worn out, and I was suffering a deep depression. Lost, I tried to escape, and I spent seven years in the wilderness. I squandered our inheritance, I bought and sold houses. I moved five times in six years. I bought luxury cars that were unable to fill the huge void Anne, my wife, had left behind. I suppose this sense of loss wasn't helped by losing faith in God. God could only play catch up when I was in this state."

I give a deep sigh.

I have come to the hard part.

"One day, feeling more desperate than ever, and now feeling suicidal, I went into a village church and asked for God's help. There was no answer. I felt alone. A week later, I went back, and I started to pray. I strongly heard a voice. 'Go home, your daughter needs you, and you need her love.' So I couldn't ignore it. I returned home to Bath and rejoined the church I'd abandoned. Shortly after that, I went on a pilgrimage to Assisi. I returned refreshed, healed, forgiven by God and ready to start a new life of love, joy and understanding. I was ready to walk beside Jesus and I was filled with the Holy Spirit."

I looked at the smiling faces before me.

"The Prodigal Son had come home."

Eighty-Two

Feeling Joy and the Power of Connection

Present Day

I WRITE THIS STARING OUT OVER THE GARDEN. A small robin hops amongst the fallen leaves, picking up small twigs and discarding them. The sky is blue today, although I felt an autumnal chill in the air on my way to the gym this morning.

I have an indescribable feeling in my chest. I have carried the burden of grief for so long, I think it will always be part of me. Pauline has made that grief shrink to manageable levels. I identify the feeling. I'm feeling joy. Something I never thought I would experience again.

I think again about how lucky I was to find Pauline, and to get a second chance after the darkness of my wilderness years. There will be many like me who don't or can't find love in later life. Or experience solace in faith, in the way I have. They will find their path to joy in other activities: fishing, sewing, watching films or TV. There is always something if you allow yourself to look hard enough to find it.

I also think about other pleasures to be found outside of finding faith or finding love. When you are grieving deeply, everything seems difficult. Connecting with people is hard. Now I am coming through to the other side, where my sorrow isn't all-consuming, I find joy in more and more things. I am in my golden years, so perhaps I search for pleasure in the simple things more than most. Experience has told me that's where the good feelings lie. A great cup of coffee; a smile and a good morning from a friendly neighbour; the song of a hopping robin.

Today I have a nice story to tell about the joy of connection.

I walk to my local Waitrose every day. It gets me out of the house, and I enjoy the fresh air and exercise. Bath is a beautiful city to wander through, and I feel gratitude for living in such a beautiful part of the country, with the soft glow of the building stock and the glorious architecture.

Pauline and I like to eat fish. It's healthy and easy to cook. We like to get our fresh fish from the counter at Waitrose. Over the years I have come to see the same people, and I always stop and have a little chat. There is one chap behind the counter who never says very much. I have stopped attempting to engage with him, accepting that he is a quiet sort.

This morning, he asks me, "What would you like today, sir?"

It's the usual question. I point at a couple of bright-eyed sea bream, laid on their bed of sparkling ice, and as I point to the fish I want, he says, out of the blue, "So what are you up to for the rest of the day?"

I nearly drop my card in surprise. He has never asked me a question beyond my choice for the catch of the day.

"Oh! I am actually going to a course on Christianity," I say. I don't expect any more than the usual polite, "Ahh," in response. Instead, I see his eyes light up. He asks me what the course entails. Then another question. Soon they are coming thick and fast. We spend a few minutes chatting about the course and what I have gained from it. We say our goodbyes, and I leave clutching my fish supper, a fullness in my heart I hadn't expected to feel today.

I think of him as I walk home, back up the steep hill. I have experienced today what it was like to have a true spontaneous connection with a stranger. Someone familiar to me but who had never shown interest in me before.

If I'm honest, I am hesitant to talk about my faith with people or discuss the Christian course I attend. I fear it might be an off-putting subject to those who might not share my beliefs. With today's surprising chat, I might rethink this.

I vow to share my experiences more freely. I can't get the look of delight in the fishmonger's eyes out of my mind. It makes me reflect that there are people out there just looking for a subject to talk about. Shyness, personal issues, whatever the reason… it's always worth striking up a conversation with someone. It might come at a time when they most need it.

I think about when else I have done this. My mind immediately alights on someone. I have the most wonderful friendship with the fellow who tests my hearing. It's a true pleasure going to visit him. He asks me about my reading at the Abbey, and then goes home and reads it himself. The next time I go, we discuss it. His interest in what I do, and the things I learn, is extremely motivating. I like to think that I add as much to his life as he does to mine through our warm and wonderful conversations.

It's amazing to me that I can talk about my life, and my faith to complete strangers who then become friends. This is a message that we can all do this. It's nothing special to me personally. We have lost our way in connecting with people; loneliness is a very real problem in this society. The number of lonely people who don't speak to anyone from one week to the next is heartbreaking. It is by sheer luck that I don't find myself alone. If I hadn't found that connection with my wonderful Pauline, I might well have been one of those statistics.

If I can do my small part, then I will.

Epilogue

When I reflect on my 'Journey Through Grief' I am reminded of the words of St Paul.

"When I am weak, then I am strong."

I imagine St Paul mulling these words over, realising their truth, during one of his many spells in prison when he was being persecuted and tortured for his Christian faith. I feel his fear and resolution as purely as if I were him.

There have been many parallels and comforts I have taken from the teachings of St Paul. At the time of deep crisis in my life, I couldn't grasp the extent of my weaknesses, and I struggled to acknowledge the fact that I had strayed, I was the proverbial lost sheep. I was unable to accept the glaring fact that I was to blame for the damage I was causing to myself and, more distressingly, to my family and friends.

There were many times I felt broken in mind, body and soul, and could not see how I would be able to rebuild. I didn't realise at the time that I could only do this one pillar at a time. It was an impossible task to try and build all three in one go. I needed the foundation of a strong mind first, then my soul and finally my body.

I see many echoes of my return from the wilderness, and now what it is like to be 'lost and found'. Hopefully I can share the understanding of what God wants us to do with our lives, and how we can share our thoughts with others, whether they are Christians or non-believers. It doesn't matter at the end of the day.

There are many people who have no faith but live full lives with their acts of giving, kindness, friendship, love and helping others. They are living out the role of a Christian. On the other hand, there are many others who think themselves Christian, worship every Sunday, but have been unable to find their true faith.

Whoever we are – Jew, Gentile or Pharisee – we should love our neighbour as ourselves. If only this message could be spread and become truth in this fragile and volatile world in which we live.

Life is so different for me now.

I will always remember the words Anne said to me when she was training to become a Relate marriage counsellor.

"I have been broken into small pieces by the tutors. This is the only way you find out who you really are. Only then can you understand the suffering of your clients and help them to lead a normal life again."

Those words resonated with me then, as they do now. I thought Anne had been so brave to go through that, in order to help those suffering. When I went through my own therapy years later, I too was broken into small pieces.

I had to break myself. Get to know the man I truly was. I had to face the truth of what I had done to others. Most importantly, it was necessary to confront the man I had been, and the life I had nearly snuffed out. My life now is so immeasurably different; it frightens me that I had let my despair get to such levels.

I am now able to understand the harm I caused and feel guilt for my actions. But with that I can also forgive myself and that has been a huge part of my healing. Through a combination of luck, counselling and the wonderful support of family, I have found the determination to put the past aside and start a new life. I have come out the other side, grateful for my life and all the blessings in it, and I can now allow myself to enjoy this second chance.

Five years ago, before I married my present wife, she asked me a searching question:

"In view of all that you have been through, and your deep depression, are you ready for another committed relationship?"

We were very much in love, and this question caught me by surprise. A few years ago, I couldn't have answered this question honestly or with an openness we have committed to each other ever since.

I feel fortunate to have had all these second chances. It could have gone very differently. It is for this reason I decided to tell my story. I wanted to engage with those who understand my journey and may have been on a journey through grief themselves.

I have been lucky. I know this. But I would like to reach out to the less fortunate, those who find themselves in troubled times; bereavement, depression, breakdown of a relationship, loneliness, homelessness, sickness, sadness or simply who are bewildered in this fragile world. I hope I can offer some words of encouragement.

I hope my story shows that things can change, and that if you stay in the day, you can always find light.